HANDS & MINDS

A GUIDE TO PROJECT-BASED LEARNING FOR TEACHERS BY TEACHERS

EDITED BY
TOM FEHRENBACHER
RANDY SCHERER

Hands and Minds: A Guide to Project-Based Learning for Teachers by Teachers

Copyright © 2017 by High Tech High

This work was made possible by the California Career Pathways Trust and the California Department of Education

Publisher: Randy Scherer
Editors: Tom Fehrenbacher and Randy Scherer
Cover design and book design by Enrique Lugo

Featuring research and writing by High Tech High educators: Alec Patton, Kelly Williams, Michelle Sadrena Clark, Colleen Green, Sarah Strong, and Peter Jana

Published by High Tech High
Distributed by High Tech High and the High Tech High Graduate School of Education

High Tech High
2861 Womble Road
San Diego, CA 92106

High Tech High Graduate School of Education
2150 Cushing Road
San Diego, CA 92106

www.hightechhigh.org
gse.hightechhigh.org

HANDS & MINDS

A GUIDE TO
PROJECT-BASED LEARNING
FOR TEACHERS BY TEACHERS

EDITED BY
TOM FEHRENBACHER
RANDY SCHERER

TABLE OF CONTENTS

PREFACE

RANDY SCHERER
CALIFORNIA CAREER PATHWAYS PBL LEADERSHIP ACADEMY

I n the spring of 2015, the California Department of Education's California Career Pathways Trust (CCPT) partnered with High Tech High Schools (HTH) to develop and implement a new professional education program for teams of educators from schools, districts, and counties across the state of California that had won CCPT grants.

Beginning in 2014, CCPT grants were awarded in two rounds over two years to support the development of educational programs designed to facilitate student access to high-skill and high-wage jobs in growing or emerging sectors of local and regional economies. CCPT grantees implemented or expanded a wide range of programs: internships, externships, and related work-based learning efforts; professional development for educators; and work to develop project-based learning methodologies in a variety of contexts. The CCPT community recognized that project-based learning holds the potential to achieve many of the goals of career technical education and of traditionally "academic" classes, by offering educational experiences that are rich in academic content and skills, connections to communities beyond school, and opportunities to enter postsecondary education and employment.

Broadly speaking, project-based learning is an educational approach that engages educators and students in authentic work that is grounded in real-world contexts, and demands real-world solutions. Work of this nature necessarily continues for an extended period of time—a class may spend weeks, months, or even years pursuing a single complex, challenging question. Students and teachers address questions such as "Why is there gun violence in our community and what should we do about it?" or "How can we teach others about what lives in our environment?" To answer these questions students may work in one class or many, and they can acquire broad and deep content knowledge and myriad skills at essentially any age level (or even in multi-age groups). For example, kindergartners, middle schoolers, or high school students may teach others what lives in the environment near their school by creating field guides of the local flora and fauna with their scientific drawings of plants and animals, along with their descriptions of what they discover—just as wildlife biologists do. In project-based learning, students do not simply learn about a subject, they become someone: students making a field guide are not just learning about the environment, they become environmental scientists and journalists, and the rigor of their work is measured according to how closely they adhere to adult or professional standards in the field.

At HTH, project-based learning is used as a methodology to achieve equity in the classroom. Because projects have multiple entry points for students and demand varying skills and knowledge, a diverse cohort of students can engage in shared work. Their differences in past academic histories and personal interests do not stop them from working together in the same classroom; diversity is an advantage, as students contribute new perspectives, bring new skills, and open new avenues for learning.

HTH was developed by a coalition of educational, civic, and business leaders in San Diego, and opened as a single high school in September 2000 with plans to serve approximately 450 students and act as an incubator for best practices in education. High Tech High is guided by four connected design principles—equity, personalization, authentic work, and collaborative design—that set aspirational goals and create a foundation for HTH's approach to teaching and learning. HTH has evolved into an integrated network that includes 13 schools on three campuses serving more than 5,300 students in grades K–12, and an adult-learning environments that includes a Teacher Credentialing Program, and the High Tech High Graduate School of Education, which offers masters' degree and professional development programs serving educators from the region, the nation, and around the world.

The PBL Leadership Academy brought together several elements of HTH-facilitated professional development:

- PBL Leadership Academy participants worked through one school year in small teams dedicated to addressing authentic needs in their local context through a leadership project.

- Participants attended multi-day Leadership Institutes at the HTH Forum and in HTH schools in the fall and spring. The Leadership Institutes featured interactive workshops led by HTH staff and students, and nationally-known guest faculty.

- Each PBL Leadership Academy team was supported by a Team Mentor, who is a practicing HTH teacher, and an expert in their subject matter and in project-based learning.

- Team Mentors made multi-day visits to their teams' schools to facilitate a variety of professional development activities. Some hosted large events featuring workshops in PBL practices for teachers from across a school, district, or even a county, while others led smaller sessions focused on supporting the specific projects of their team. Team members and their mentors co-designed the visits.

- The PBL Leadership Academy staff curated a variety of online resources, and participant teams met with their HTH Team Mentor regularly online for planning sessions, critiques, and project reflections.

The work of the educators who participated in the PBL Leadership Academy, and in broader CCPT efforts, is presented in two publications: *Hands and Minds: A Guide to Project-Based Learning for Teachers by Teachers* and the accompanying volume *Inspiration, Not Replication: How Teachers Are Leading School Change From the Inside.* The first is a guide to the methodologies of project-based learning; the second captures stories of the educators who embarked on journeys of transformation, of their classrooms, schools, and themselves.

These books were created by HTH educators—their research comes from their classrooms, their schools, their experiences as mentors to educators in the PBL Leadership Academy, site visits to PBL Leadership Academy schools across California, and interviews with nationally known experts and the teachers and students in these books (student names contained in these publications are pseudonyms).

The two volumes, *Hands and Minds and Inspiration, Not Replication* are complementary, and may be read separately or together in any order. Just as the work of the hand cannot be separated from that of the mind, the methods that educators and students use in project-based learning cannot be separated from their personal stories. We hope that many educators, students, and families will see themselves and their own schools in these pages, and that they will be inspired and aided in continuing to create and recreate those schools.

INTRODUCTION

PROJECT-BASED CURRICULUM DESIGN: ESSENTIAL PRACTICES

TOM FEHERENBACHER
HIGH TECH HIGH, NEW TEACHER CREDENTIALING INSTRUCTOR

California Career Pathways Project Based Learning (PBL) Leadership Academy participants worked in teams to design and implement original project-based learning curricula in schools across the state—their methods can be brought to seemingly any school, and are curated here, in *Hands and Minds: A Guide to Project-Based Learning for Teachers by Teachers* and the accompanying volume *Inspiration, Not Replication: How Teachers Are Leading School Change From the Inside*. Both books show a remarkable thing happening: a community of schools across California working to uncover what works in schools, and how to make that happen more broadly.

Written by six teachers at various High Tech High schools, *Hands and Minds: A Guide to Project-Based Learning for Teachers by Teachers* shares recipes for setting up project based learning in the classroom. Project-based teachers from across California contributed to this work. Together, these teachers laid out their best practices and made clear their reasons for doing so. Project-based teachers want to tell a story, which like many stories, starts with a problem and ends with a solution. Most of the classroom action takes place in between, when students are working on the problem and developing a solution worthy of public presentation.

To do this well, teachers in project-based learning classes embrace specific practices to engage all students from the start, facilitate growth and mastery of core academic content and important skills tied to deeper learning, integrate school with the community, showcase products and processes to authentic audiences beyond an individual teacher, and engage in meaningful assessment and reflection. PBL teachers want permeable boundaries between the school and the community—students regularly venture into the community for fieldwork, internships, exhibitions of learning, and more, and the community ventures into the school for similar work. PBL teachers want students to make a story that captures the community's attention.

This practitioner's *Guide* shows how to go about this from the teacher's point of view: how to plan a project, how to make student work public, how to develop a culture of critique, how to engage in community partnerships, how to change assessment practices, and how to use reflection to integrate hands and minds. This *Guide* is for the educator, student, or parent who is not willing to wait for institutions to change; this book is for those who believe, "we can do this."

In **Alec Patton's** "How to Get Started in a Project" the author provides a clear view of planning and launching projects. Patton's step-by-step approach comes complete with all the considerations any project implementer might need to know. At times, Patton cautions, "don't do that," and he shares ways to avoid common pitfalls in the early stages of PBL. Patton shows the reader, "Here is how *you* can do this!"

In "Making Student Learning Public," **Kelly Williams** goes into the details of putting on an exhibition, holding presentations of learning, and successfully completing student-led conferences. She shares how to structure and facilitate each type of public presentation, where it can take place, who is involved, and what their roles will be.

Michelle Sadrena Clark's chapter, "Critique and Revision" looks at the importance of critique in project based learning. Clark finds it essential to set up a positive classroom culture around critique. She shows how classroom dynamics and student personalities become powerful contributors through norms and protocols. Clark shares the "how to" of critique, finding students who participate in critique are better prepared for life.

In **Colleen Green's** chapter, "Community Partnerships," the author explores service learning, internships, and externships. Green shows how this work has positive impacts on both the student and community partner. This happens best when the community partners needs are addressed, the students interests are met, and common ground is found in the curriculum. Green lays out the plans for gearing up, running down the road, and sharing memories afterward.

Sarah Strong flips conventional classroom assessment on its head. In her chapter, "Student Centered Assessment," Strong shows how students and teachers can do far more than meet the expectations of tests. Teachers can facilitate student ownership of assessment and the results are powerful. Strong's chapter is packed with strategies which help students design their own learning goals, assess with their peers, and use dialogue to find where their work can be improved.

In the closing chapter, "Reflection," **Peter Jana** takes on one of the buzzwords in education. Jana's take on the word will come as a surprise to many. In his examination, Jana doesn't kill the patient but brings it back to life. He finds that reflection truly is the basis of learning. And, as things turn out, doing reflection right takes careful consideration, planning big and small, and a rich variety of experiences. Jana explains it all, providing three case studies which catch reflection in the act. It turns out that projects do reflection best.

In many ways, each of the chapters in this guide connect to one another. In project based learning, the student's work coalesces around exhibitions, community partnership experiences, critique and assessment innovation, and the project itself. An internship may allow students to explore the workplace, but it also serves as opportunity for students to reflect upon his or her experiences daily through written blog posts which can later used in the students' presentations of learning. There is a natural overlap in the "content" of project based learning which, once started, reinforces and builds upon itself. The authors reference these connections and point out their importance. But, each author, also, applies a specific lens to project-based learning and, in so doing outlines the essential points and details which make project-based learning possible from any chapter's vantage point.

This *Guide* is like a cookbook, and the schools referenced within it are test kitchens. All the chapters share recipes which come complete with an analyses of specific PBL ingredients, explorations of particular methods, and examples of products well-baked. There is still testing to be done—on infusing new or different content standards in projects, broadening the role of an exhibition's audience, thoughtfully using community feedback in the school, getting closer to reality in assessment, or making academic work more interdisciplinary.

Hands and Minds: A Guide to Project-Based Learning for Teachers by Teachers shows that PBL is not always about the perfect project, the great problems solved, or the complete internship. It isn't always about when the rocket blasts off or the audience applauds. PBL has a daily life. It's about seeing the work through, even in the last days before the exhibition. It's about getting along with the group, or figuring how to. It's about looking at the work seriously for what really matters and taking that to heart.

PROJECTS ARE DESIGNED TO BE ENGAGING, ACTIVE EXPERIENCES WITH MULTIPLE ENTRY POINTS FOR DIVERSE LEARNERS THAT INVITE MULTIPLE PERSPECTIVES AND FOSTER DIVERSE, INNOVATIVE THINKING.

CHAPTER 1

GETTING STARTED

BY ALEC PATTON, PH.D.
HIGH TECH HIGH CHULA VISTA

WHERE DO PROJECT IDEAS COME FROM?

A group of high school seniors conceives of and performs a play about the aftermath of the death of Michael Brown in Ferguson, Missouri. Middle school students design, build and fly tiny drones through an obstacle course. Elementary students document the presence of a specific species of salamander in an area near school where they have never been identified before, and they implement a novel solution to sustain the population. A group of high school juniors teams up with a post-doc researcher in marine biology to run the largest-ever laboratory study of coral. Sixth graders design and build tiny houses in the lot of an old warehouse where local artists can live and work. Elementary schoolers grow produce in an urban garden, publish a cookbook of affordable, nutritious, locally sourced meals, and learn to cook their favorites.

The idea that such a diverse range of work all fits under the banner of "project-based learning" (PBL), on the face of it, can stretch the imagination. But strip away the specifics of content knowledge and production methods from any of these examples, and there is consistent basic structure: questions worth pursuing, worthwhile learning goals, a sequence of multiple drafts and critique, frequent opportunities for myriad forms of assessment and reflection, and a public exhibition of learning. These steps are as consistent as the chords of a twelve bar blues, though, as with the blues, every teacher's approach is unique.

To discover their own projects, teachers begin by connecting with their—and their students'—passions. Teachers who are seeking to engage in project-based learning inquire of themselves and their students: "What do you love to do? What do you wish you knew how to do? What you worry about, and what problems do you want to solve? What do you want to contribute to your community? What do you hope every student will be able to experience?"

There, in the things teachers and students care about most, are the seeds of projects.

Specifically, the seed of a project could be...

A QUESTION:
Effective questions have multiple answers and myriad angles that appeal to different people and invite diverse thinking. For example, "How can we decide which news to trust?"

A LOCAL (OR GLOBAL) PROBLEM THAT YOU AND YOUR STUDENTS CAN ADDRESS OR SOLVE:
Be sure to choose a social issue worthy of exploration and relatable to the kids' lives. For example, "What can we do to help stop gun violence in our community?"

A THING YOU WANT TO MAKE; A PRODUCT:
For example, a photography book, a pop-up restaurant, robots or a tiny house.

A POTENTIAL COLLABORATOR OR CLIENT:
For example, a local community center that is in need of renovations.

AN EXHIBITION VENUE:
For example, a local cafe that is interested in displaying student work.

AN EXISTING PROJECT YOU WANT TO ADAPT.

There are an increasing number of projects online—good places to start are the High Tech High Project Cards found at hightechhigh.org/unboxed and Models of Excellence: The Center for High Quality Student Work, found at: modelsofexcellence.org

STUDENT IDEAS AND INTERESTS:

Ask your students what they're passionate about! They have great ideas about their own learning and the needs that they see in the community.

Over time, teachers discover that their "project sense" is impossible to turn off: they see projects in parks and art galleries, but also at the grocery store, in the car, and on TV. Just as photographers see the world as potential images to be framed, and engineers see mechanical problems to be solved, teachers who do project-based learning see a world full of projects.

This initial "spark" of passion is critical to a project's ultimate success. Of course, projects depend on much more than passion alone, but without passion, the project will be less engaging for everyone, and the quality of students' work will reflect that.

TO WORK ALONE OR COLLABORATE—THAT IS THE QUESTION!

Collaborating with a colleague on a project can be immensely satisfying: it allows teachers to share their different perspectives, their different skills, their different relationships with the students, and, perhaps most useful, collaborative relationships give each teacher a support systems and even someone to ask "is this a crazy idea?"

If you are deciding whether or not to co-design a project with a colleague, here are some questions to consider and discuss with colleagues:

1. What is each teacher's vision for the project? What does each teacher have in common with a potential partner? How will working together be positive experience?

2. How much class time is each teacher able to devote to this project? (Which class periods are available, which days of the week, and which weeks in the semester).

3. When will the team be able to meet to plan collaboratively, both before and during the project?

4. How many students in total will be a part of this project?

5. What will students learn that will be meaningful for each teacher's class?

6. Which pieces of the project is each teacher responsible for? Will this work for each?

7. What can we do to work well together if our classrooms are not close?

8. How can we collaborate even if we don't share students? Can one class design the product, while another builds it? Can one class create a product and another class uses it? What examples of client and consumer or designer and builder can we use?

"COLLABORATIVE" AND "INTERDISCIPLINARY" ARE NOT THE SAME THING

In project-based learning, people tend to use the word "interdisciplinary" to refer to projects that are co-designed by teachers of different subjects, but this is not strictly accurate. In fact, all projects can be interdisciplinary, if they are designed like the work that professionals do, which does not divide neatly into categories like "Social Studies," "Math," or "Chemistry." These categories may be a convenient filing system for human knowledge, but once students enter the workplace—and once they enter the world of project-based learning—it is likely that nothing they do will ever divide neatly into these categories ever again.

Other projects might have more than one teacher involved in their creation and delivery, but the work completed by each may be only sequential and potentially even unrelated. Truly interdisciplinary projects are dependent upon a conversation taking place between teachers and disciplines. In interdisciplinary projects, the disciplinary focus represented by each teacher informs and can even impact the other. Participating in such interdisciplinary work, can energize, challenge and intellectually fruitful for teachers.

DESIGN YOUR PROJECT

A PROJECT HAS THREE BASIC DRIVERS:

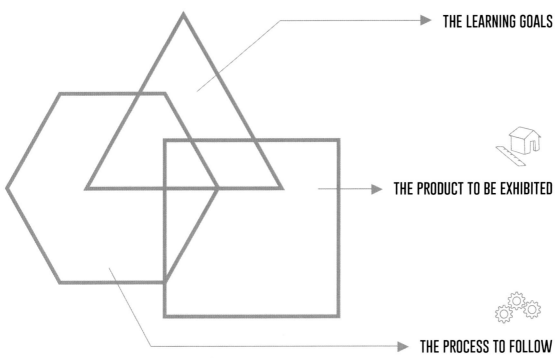

THE LEARNING GOALS

THE PRODUCT TO BE EXHIBITED

THE PROCESS TO FOLLOW

An individual teacher's project design might begin with any one of these, but ultimately, all three must be addressed.

DETERMINE LEARNING GOALS

It's no secret that many teachers are expected to cover an immense number of standards. Just to be clear, a project may cover a large number of content standards, but that is not the point of project-based learning, any more than professionals draw on a wide breadth of shallow knowledge when they are doing a project.

By choosing content and performance standards thoughtfully, and pursuing them in depth via rigorous projects, teachers facilitate student mastery of content and skills which have broad applications across the subject domain.

One way to choose which standards to focus on in a particular project is to ask yourself "What on this list of standards speaks to the true essence of my discipline?" Whatever standards go on that list are the ones that matter—these are what EL Education Chief Academic Officer Ron Berger calls the "Power Standards."[1]

Another way to articulate the academic knowledge inherent in a project is to imagine a need in the community or a product that students will make. What will the students need to learn in order to solve a problem in the community? What will students need to learn in order to create a specific product? These are equally valid paths to discovering the academics inherent in project-based learning.

Once you have a list of "power standards," it's time to figure out which of these standards the students will learn through the project you're designing. One activity that is helpful is to prioritize your learning goals for students into three categories—when doing so, think of your values as an educator, the standards of your discipline and school, relevant professional skills, and your students' interests or needs:

WHAT ARE THE ENDURING UNDERSTANDINGS SOUGHT THROUGH THIS PROJECT?
What is most important to teach and learn? What are the essential questions?
Focus on one or two fundamental reasons why students do this project.

WHAT IS IMPORTANT TO KNOW AND/OR DO?
What are good things for the students to practice?
Establish three to five important ideas and skills that students will regularly practice and master.

WHAT IS WORTH BEING FAMILIAR WITH?
What are good things for students to see, to hear about, and to try? What are students exposed to in this project?

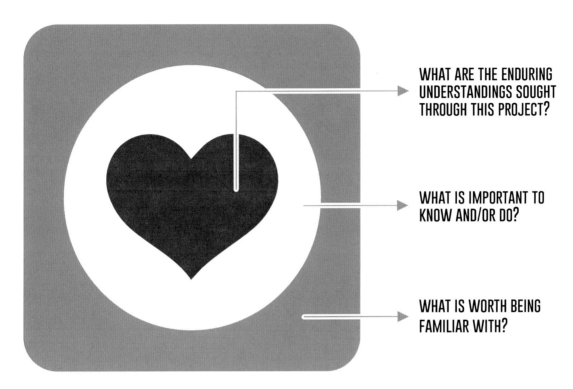

WHAT ARE THE ENDURING UNDERSTANDINGS SOUGHT THROUGH THIS PROJECT?

WHAT IS IMPORTANT TO KNOW AND/OR DO?

WHAT IS WORTH BEING FAMILIAR WITH?

Think of as much as you like here—these are ideas that are students will become aware of, and begin to understand, but are not prioritized as the essential core of the project, nor are they the key learnings that students will hold, perhaps for the rest of their lives, after doing this project.

Once you've refined your ideas for learning goals, think about how they can be expressed in language that is student-friendly, open-ended, and likely to become part of students' everyday conversations.

LEARNING GOALS EXPRESSED IN STUDENT FRIENDLY LANGUAGE:

"By the end of this project each one of us will be an expert on the Syrian refugee crisis, to the extent that we could each handle being interviewed about it on the radio like it was no big deal."

A word about project-based learning with different ages: Much of the core practices in project-based learning are equally valid with early elementary school students and high school or even college students, as well as everyone in between. A project that challenges students to create and publish an original field guide to the local flora and fauna in the community around the school can be done—and has been done—at nearly every level of school, as have rocketry projects, nutrition projects, projects to help the homeless, projects to document personal histories of veterans, projects to improve community facilities and many more. The core practices of learning by doing, bringing hands and minds together to create meaningful products for real audiences, and sharing student learning in a variety of contexts have inherent value to all students.

However, teachers in elementary school must be sure that they plan for important skill acquisition, such as early literacy development, and be conscious of the developmental levels of their students. And all teachers should ensure that project-based learning is academically relevant—for example, if the math class is involved in the field guide project, high school seniors should do more than simple species counts with their math teacher!

DESIGNING THE ESSENTIAL QUESTION

Essential questions are open-ended points of inquiry—relevant to academia, students' lives and the world beyond school—expressed in student-friendly language. They are designed to encourage diverse thinking and further inquiry. Essential questions can come from students or teachers, can be created at various points in the planning processes, and can be revised and revisited throughout a project. Essential questions often appear simple, but encourage multidisciplinary thinking, deep inquiry, rigorous reflection, and even differing conclusions as students explore alternative, personally relevant answers.[2]

A well-crafted essential question requires students to conduct serious research, and also inspires conversations among friends at lunch or among family at dinner. Create authentic ways for students to easily refer to the essential question throughout the project.

A POWERFUL ESSENTIAL QUESTION:

- Provokes diverse, innovative thought and layers of inquiry.

- Has no easy answer.

- Captures students' imaginations.

- Can be asked in the world of work, academics and personal or family life.

EXAMPLES OF ESSENTIAL QUESTIONS:

- What does it mean to act like a girl?

- How safe is it to swim in the ocean today?

- What should I eat and why?

- Why is _____ happening and what should we do about it?

While an essential question may be there from the start, refinements to the essential question may also take place later. In fact, some of the most intriguing layers to an essential question emerge when students ask their own questions about a controversial issue as part of a project launch. Individual students or groups may also be asked to craft individualized research questions related to a larger essential question that encompasses the work of the whole class. A newer, more subtle version of the essential question may evolve as ongoing research and information shed light upon the older question.

As you come up with an essential question, consider how much cognitive work you want the question to do for students, and how much you want them to do themselves. For example, the question "how can we help integrate refugees into our community?" assumes that the more fundamental question "should America be taking in refugees?" has already been answered—therefore, a great deal of thinking has been done for the students before the project starts—and a student who doesn't agree that America should be taking in refugees has no entry point for the project. A good essential question for a project like this may be "Why is there a refugee crisis and what should we do about it?"

DESIGNING THE PRODUCT

The product is often what distinguishes project-based learning from other education methods—but be careful: project-based learning is about more than just making fancy stuff. The product, and the audience it is intended for, provides a focus for student work from the beginning, and students continue to develop it over multiple drafts, until they have created something worth of exhibiting. And, well-designed products demand that students discover, practice and master a variety of skills and content in order to create them; exhibitions of student learning motivate critique, revision, deeper learning and ongoing reflection.

There are generally four types of products found in project-based learning classes:

1. An object that is either tangible or digital

2. A performance

3. A service

4. An implementable solution to a problem

For example:

 PROJECT-BASED LEARNING GUIDED BY THE CREATION OF AN OBJECT:

Staircases to Nowhere
Andrew Gloag, Physics, High Tech High
Jeff Robin, Art, High Tech High

To understand the intersection between physics, math, engineering, and the arts, students designed and built staircases to nowhere. Students began by individually exploring, measuring, and documenting existing staircases and then playing with materials and their imaginations to design and build a 1:10 scale staircase by themselves. With a partner, using trigonometry and computer-aided design, they created and built a 1:5 scale staircase. Students selected specific design ideas and in a group of ten they created life size staircases to nowhere at various locations in the school. Students photographed every staircase that they built, saved all of their math and physics classwork and related blueprints, and published a book that documents the project. The model staircases are displayed in the hallways with posters showcasing the blueprints, physics and math, and the full sized staircases became an element of the school's physical campus.

A PERFORMANCE:

#Ferguson
Matt Simon, Humanities, High Tech High Chula Vista

After studying a number of different current events, students in Matt Simon's class decided to write a play focusing on a specific current event: the protests in Ferguson, Missouri, following the shooting of Michael Brown by a police officer. In order to create the play, students listed characters necessary to provide a multiple perspectives on what happened in Ferguson and what the root causes were. Next, they made a timeline of events from Brown's death to the grand jury decision not to indict the police officer. Students worked in teams to write three scenes per team following the same characters through the timeline. The result was a play that combined multiple intertwining stories and perspectives on a controversial news story

A SERVICE:

Trout in the Classroom
Shelley Glenn Lee, Science, High Tech Elementary North County
Chris Olivas, Physical Science, High Tech Middle North County
Johnnie Lymann, Chemistry, High Tech High North County
Matt Leader, Biology, High Tech High North County

Students at High Tech Elementary, Middle, and High North County developed interdisciplinary projects based on "Trout in the Classroom," a national project in which students work with their regional Fish and Wildlife Service to raise trout eggs for later release into a local approved freshwater habitat, in an attempt to restore native fish populations in rivers, creeks and watersheds. Elementary, middle, and high students partnered with the Escondido Creek Conservancy and California Fish and Wildlife to raise trout on campus with tanks placed at each school. Each of these science classes worked with other partner classes on projects that aligned service learning with necessary academic curricula. Third graders integrated this experience into their "Great Migrations" project in which they learned about why animals migrate and created maps of local animal migrations. Eighth graders integrated Trout in the Classroom into their "Ripple Effect" project in which they learned about local and global oceanic ecosystems, ocean acidification, and plastic contamination in the ocean. In addition to raising trout in the classroom, they worked to reduce plastic waste by placing water bottle filling stations on campus. Tenth graders learned about water's role in moving other chemicals through local ecosystems and how to test for levels of specific nutrients and pollutants, and created a website to help other schools do this project. Eleventh graders collaborated with local biologists to study and publish their research into the genetics, anatomy, physiology, evolutionary history, and conservation of Southern Steelhead Trout. All of these students raised Rainbow/ Steelhead Trout in their classes and released them into approved local waterways as part of larger effort to reintroduce these trout to the watershed.

AN IMPLEMENTABLE SOLUTION TO A PROBLEM:

The ReVision Project,
John Bosselman, English, High Tech High Chula Vista
Megan Willis, Engineering, High Tech High Chula Vista

The ReVision Project is a consultation and design firm run by 50 twelfth-grade students and two teachers. In the 2015/16 school year, ReVision worked with eight clients in the community on a number of different design challenges, ranging from engineering a system to divert trash from the Tijuana Estuary to designing an outdoor coffee shop in the back of a thrift store.

In order to design solutions to these complex issues, students used architectural and visual design strategies, together with human-centered design processes, to create solutions to challenges faced by non-profits, charities, small business, and local government.

CONNECT LEARNING GOALS AND PRODUCTS

In all these cases, the project comes to life because students feel an authentic need to master thoughtfully selected learning goals in their quest to create meaningful and beautiful work.

If a teacher starts planning a project with an idea for a product, showcase event or performance, or other end result in mind, it's a good idea to make a prototype as soon as possible—and to reverse engineer it to understand the learning goals inherent in it's creation.

But if a teacher begins planning by first naming what the students should learn, coming up with the end product or exhibition event takes some more thinking. I was in this situation when I decided to do a project in which students gained an in-depth understanding of the Syrian refugee crisis, and again the following year when I wanted students to learn to assess the credibility of news sources. In both instances, the learning goal preceded the product, and as a result, I had to create prototypes of multiple products until I found the one that worked well for my students, our resources, and my strengths as a teacher.

In the cases where teachers have a learning goal, but no product, they might ask themselves the following questions.

IN WHAT PROFESSIONS WOULD YOU NEED TO GAIN EXPERTISE IN THIS?

Any valuable learning goal will have application in the adult world outside school. Therefore, a good first step to coming up with a meaningful product is to think about the professions where this learning goal is relevant.

At Morro Bay High School, teachers were excited to teach students about the people, geography and economy of the local agricultural community in San Luis Obispo.

Professionals who would likely work on a project like this include:

- Journalists
- Economists
- Farmers, Vintners, and Agricultural Workers
- Ethnographers
- Geographers
- Photographers or Videographers
- Graphic Designers
- Publishers & Editors
- Marketing Teams
- Business People
- Local Politicians
- Local Chamber of Commerce
- Local Tourism Bureau

WHAT PROJECTS WOULD A PROFESSIONAL DO?

Now that you have a list of professions that use this type of knowledge, brainstorm the products that these professionals would make in order to share their learning.

- Journalists: Articles, TV or radio news reports, infographics, panel discussions, podcasts, documentary films, oral history interviews. Additionally, journalists would likely work with many local experts, as well as publishers, editors, graphic designers, photographers and videographers.
- Economists: Original economic research, reports, media appearances.
- Farmers, Vintners, and Agricultural Workers: Informed decisions about future produce and business, as well as products for sale. Additionally, they might collaborate with marketing teams, graphic designers and local business people.

- Ethnographers: Original research into people and cultures, articles, media products.
- Geographers: Original research into people and places, articles, work with local government, media products.
- Biologists: Consult with local agricultural workers, products to help agricultural yield, scientific testing.
- Chemists: Pesticides and herbicides, or natural products that achieve these results without harmful effects.
- Photographers or Videographers: Documentary image creation, story development, museum installations, media products.
- Graphic Designers: Various media products for journalists as well as for the local business community.
- Local Politicians: Campaigns, new laws, new land use or zoning regulations, voter registration drives.
- Local Chamber of Commerce: Decision and media products that support local businesses.
- Local Tourism Bureau: Marketing plans, media products, tours, etc.
- Activists: Community service, fundraisers, protests, media appearances, campaigns, voter registration drives.

WHAT ARE THE TEACHERS—AND STUDENTS—MOST EXCITED ABOUT MAKING?

Do you dream of being a documentary filmmaker? Are you passionate about supporting a local issue or solving a problem in your community? How about a rocket scientist? Now is the time to connect with your own passions outside of the classroom in order to decide how to harness this energy into a project.

When you have an idea, buy some snacks and invite students to come to your room during lunch to talk about the next project. This way, you can informally share your idea and get their responses. You will probably end this lunch meeting with a better idea than you started with.

When you are ready—when you have taken steps to plan what you can, but still have important questions about what students might create, how it might be displayed or how it might be assessed—convene a group of students and/or colleagues for a Tuning Protocol.[3]

In the case described above, the teachers at Morro Bay High School consulted with students and decided to create a field guide to the agricultural community surrounding their school. The teachers and students agreed that they could be creative, have fun, do valuable original research and showcase their community, and stay true to the essence of the English class that took the lead on the project, by focusing their learning towards the creation of an original book documenting the local agricultural community.

WHO ARE OUR POTENTIAL AUDIENCES FOR THIS WORK?

The most accessible audience for a project is parents: a project in which parents' minds are changed about a serious issue because their children have made them better-informed citizens is a powerful project. A word of warning: audiences which are prestigious but remote from students' own experience can to be more exciting to the teacher than to the students.

Another accessible audience can be other students. Perhaps your students can create toys for students at a local elementary school, and learn important lessons about physics, engineering, and design in the process. Or, they might write children's books for other students, and learn about literacy strategies and narrative structure, and also serve as reading buddies along the way. Perhaps your students could teach something specific to a neighboring class, or provide something of value to another class or student group in your school.

Community groups also provide welcoming audiences for student work. A local veterans' group might want their personal histories documented. A local animal shelter may need newly constructed homes, play structures and signage for the animals in its care. An environmental group may support the creation of a field guide to the local area, and help distribute it to it's members.

Presenting work to a valued or respected audience is an extraordinary learning experience—this situates student work in the world beyond school, creates an authentic system of accountability, and motivates students to do their best because someone is waiting to receive their work.

SET A TIME AND PLACE FOR AN EXHIBITION OF STUDENT LEARNING

If students are going to be creating an amazing product, and sharing it with a real-world audience, there needs to be a time and place where this happens. This may be an open-house event at school, a gallery-style showcase event, a performance, a panel discussion, a book launch party, or a conference.

Here are three questions to ask as you decide a time and place for your exhibition of student learning:

1. Should the exhibition of student learning happen during school hours or after school?
2. Should the exhibition of student learning happen on-campus or off-campus?
3. What potential exhibition venues are there in the local community?

DO THE PROJECT YOURSELF

By making your own prototype version of the product, you will deeply understand what students will learn from making the product, whether making it was a valuable use of time, whether you were excited about doing it, what resources (tangible, social, and mental) you needed in order to do it, where you had problems, and how long it took (though remember, it will take the students much longer than it took you!).

Later, when you share your prototype with your students, you may decide as a group to take the project in a different direction from your prototype. This is valuable learning in its own right, and is much more productive than the class coming up with a project as a group without critiquing a teacher's prototype.

DOES THE TEACHER NEED TO COME UP THE PRODUCT? WHY NOT LET EVERY STUDENT COME UP WITH THEIR OWN PRODUCT?

Teachers new to project-based learning may hope to design projects in which all students learn the same content, but every student decides what product they will make on their own.

There are three good reasons not to do this:
1. If everyone is creating the same thing—even if some of the specific academic content is different—students can learn from each other's successes and mistakes. If one student is making a documentary, one is making a sculpture, and one is making a business plan, they can't learn very much from each other. However, if everyone is making simple machines, or everyone is creating documentaries about relevant social issues, students can see how their peers solve problems differently, and stay on a trajectory towards high quality work.
2. If everyone creates something different, the teacher can't make a prototype, which limits his or her ability to plan. And, because the teacher won't know the subtleties of the different processes to create each different product, it will be difficult, if not impossible, to schedule critiques, provide effective feedback, or simply have enough materials in class.
3. It's not possible to create assessment criteria that will enable students to grow as learners if that criteria needs to cover all possible products.

There are two exceptions to this:
1. If both the students and teacher feel very confident about their experiences in a project-based learning environment, and both share a coherent vision for a product that diverges from what the class is doing, it may be a good idea to give one or two students freedom to deviate from the plan. The students will be more excited about the project and their experience may help the teacher improve the project in the future. Be careful, though—there is a slippery slope to soon having all students doing their own thing.
2. Incorporating a "free choice" element into a project for honors credit can be fun and lead to some great work. Just make sure it's a dessert, not the main course.

THE PROCESSES WE WILL FOLLOW

You know your learning goals and your product. You've done the project yourself. You've provisionally come up with an essential question (though you may keep changing it as you continue to plan).

It's time to make a project plan, a timeline, and something you can share with students and parents.

MAKE A PROJECT PLAN AND A CALENDAR

There are a variety of project planners that work for different teachers. Some prefer backwards planning, thinking about the process with the goal of exhibition always in mind. Others prefer to work forwards from the learning goals and essential questions. Yet others work modularly, beginning with the pieces that they know, such as plans for critique or drafting and revision, and filling in gaps as they develop the overall project plan. Sooner or later, all teachers must commit their plan to a calendar that they will share with students, families and colleagues.

START A CALENDAR WITH TIME CONSTRAINTS AND BASIC MILESTONES

- The most basic project planning question is "How much time will we actually have to do this project?" To find out, mark the following on your calendar:

- Any days with little or no instructional time (holidays, professional days, half days, testing days, etc.).

- Exhibition day (if you start with this, you can work backwards to see how much time you need for the full project).
  - If you can, set your exhibition day a week earlier than you need to. Your first project will probably take longer than you anticipated, and you are likely to need to free up extra time late in the project.
  - Remember to build in time after exhibition to reflect on the full project.

- Any predictable delays in the project.

- For example, if you are making a book, you will need to send it to the publishers about two weeks before exhibition.
- Due dates for drafts and corresponding dates for in-class critiques and progress assessments. Use your experience doing the project yourself in order to work these out.
- The day of the project launch.

These basic milestones show how much time you have for the project, which informs all further project planning.

ONCE YOU HAVE THE BASIC MILESTONES, MOVE BACK AND FORTH BETWEEN ANY OTHER PROJECT PLANNER YOU MAY USE AND THE CALENDAR

Project planners are graphic organizers for teachers: they organize a teacher's thinking about products, content, skills, materials, process, and more—and they provides reminders of what to not forget.

The best way to use any project planner is to respond to the prompts that are relevant to your project, and ignore the ones that aren't—customize it to your needs.

As you plan, return to the calendar to add more detail. This might include the following: core academic content that students will be learning, summaries of the lessons that will take place each day, and more information about specific drafts or critiques that are due throughout the course of a project.

"BAKED-IN" EQUITY

Track the status of every student's draft using a spreadsheet, with notes to indicate what kind of support they need to advance to the next stage. Teachers can also post these types of charts publicly in the classroom, and students can help track their own progress, make notes to one another, and post questions or requests for help.

PLAN FOR MULTIPLE DRAFTS & CRITIQUE

The essence of project-based learning is the path from first idea to final product, and it's never too early for a first draft. If every student has their own piece of work to develop and refine, lessons become less abstract and more meaningful. Also, the first draft serves as a baseline for the teacher, who can use these initial drafts to identify what skills they will need to teach.

Questions to consider as you plan the sequence of the drafts:

- How soon after project launch can students make a first draft?
- Is there an opportunity for students to do an early, low-stakes "mini-version" of the product? For example, if students are making podcasts based on interviews with local community members, they could record interviews with a peer or family member in the first few days of the project; if students will make boats large enough to float teams of classmates across a nearby lake, how soon can they make a prototype that floats in a tub of water in the classroom?
- Who should see each draft?
  - The teacher may choose to critique each student's work individually. Students revise their work based on the teacher's feedback.
  - The whole class may critique one student's piece of work, so everybody learns from that student's successes (and mistakes).
    - Make sure to use a very strong piece of work for this, so the critique session doesn't become an exercise in public shaming.
  - Every student's work is critiqued by groups of other students.
  - Experts from outside the school critique a few selected pieces of work in a "master class."
- What will be your bottlenecks? How will you manage these?
  - For example: if everybody is waiting for the teacher's critique of their drafts, what happens while the students waiting for their work to be returned to them?

BAKED-IN EQUITY: EMPATHY INTERVIEWS AND STUDENT QUESTIONNAIRES

When you start dreaming up a project, ask yourself "which students will be excited to be doing this?" "Which students will have experience in their background that will set them up for success?" "Which students will need the most support in order to be successful?" Think of your students who have the most trouble connecting to what's happening in class, and ask yourself "what about this will make _____ excited to come to class every day?"

The easiest way to find out the answer to this question is to ask the student you're wondering about. Do this one-on-one, when you have time to give him or her your full attention.

A good way to get a basic sense of what every student cares about most is through a "student interests and skills questionnaire."

Questions you might want to ask include:

- What's your favorite meal?
- Do you have a computer with internet access that you can use outside of school?
- What was your favorite and least favorite parts of school? Why? Tell me the real details—the more I know about how you experience school, the better projects I can design!
- What's something you're good at that your teachers don't know about?
- Who do you want to be when you are grown up? Why?
- Do you have any health issues that I should know about?
- What do you enjoy about studying this subject? [English/Math/Science/etc.]
- What do you dislike about studying this subject? [English/Math/Science/etc.]
- What do you want to get better at in this subject this year?
- What do you spend the most time doing outside of school?

MAKE CONTACT WITH ADULTS IN THE COMMUNITY

Every project benefits from the involvement of adults other than the teacher. There are several ways that adults from the local community (and beyond) can help with a project:

- As expert advisers (for example, parents helping with construction).
- As inspiring speakers at a project launch.
- As commissioners of the work, or clients.
- As experts in a critique session.
- As expert panelists in a final assessment.

TUNING YOUR PROJECT WITH COLLEAGUES (AND STUDENTS!)

At this point, you have...

- A prototype of your final product.
- An essential question (though this is subject to change).
- A draft of a project plan (though this may have questions or incomplete sections).

It's time to "tune" your project.

A "project tuning" is a structured conversation created by five schools in the Coalition of Essential Schools and popularized by the National School Reform Faculty. In a project tuning, one teacher shares his or her project plan, along with a question or two, with a group of colleagues to seek help, advice and guidance. For example, a teacher might describe a project in which he or she knows the learning goals and the basic timeline, but is struggling to decide between possible products to create, and is questioning whether students should work in groups or alone. The group asks different types of questions and then discusses the project and the teacher's questions. The protocol has specific times and relies on a facilitator for it's success—a detailed version is provided on pages 42 and 43.

Whenever possible, invite students to take part in critique sessions—as the people who will actually be doing the project, their perspectives are extremely helpful.

PROJECT TUNING PROTOCOL

NORMS:

- Hard on the content, soft on the people
- Share the air (or "step up, step back")
- Be kind, helpful and specific

THE PROTOCOL:

OVERVIEW (5 MIN)

Presenter gives an overview of the work and explains what goals he/she had in mind when designing the project. The presenter might choose to also put the project into context so the critical friends understand how it fits into the larger scope and sequence of the class. Participants then have an opportunity to look at "the work" (e.g. project handouts, rubrics, student work, etc.). The presenter then shares a dilemma by **framing a question** for the critical friends group to address during the discussion.

CLARIFYING QUESTIONS (5 MIN)

Critical friends ask **clarifying** questions of the presenter. Clarifying questions have brief, factual answers and are intended to help the person asking the question develop a deeper understanding of the dilemma. An example of a clarifying question is "How were the groups chosen for this activity?"

PROBING QUESTIONS* (10 MIN)

Critical friends ask **probing** questions of the presenter. Probing questions help the presenter expand his/her thinking about the dilemma. However, probing questions should not be "advice in disguise", such as "Have you considered...?" Examples of probing questions are "How did each student demonstrate their understanding through the final product?" or "What evidence did you gather to determine the extent to which the goals of your project were met?"

DISCUSSION (15 MIN)

The presenter reframes the question if necessary and is then physically removed from the group. The group discusses the dilemma and attempts to provide insight on the question raised by the presenter. It may help to **begin with warm feedback,** such as "What went well with the project?" and then move on to cool feedback. Cool feedback includes a more critical analysis of the work, using the question proposed by the presenter to frame the discussion. For example, "What isn't the presenter considering?" or "I wonder what would happen if...". *The presenter does not speak during the discussion, but listen and take notes. It is a good idea for the presenter to physically sit outside of the circle and for the group to close in the circle without the presenter. Resist the urge to speak directly to the presenter. The facilitator may need to remind participants of the presenter's focusing questions. It can be helpful to ask after 5 minutes, "Are we addressing the presenter's questions?"*

RESPONSE (5 MIN)

The presenter has the opportunity to respond to the discussion. It is not necessary to respond point by point to what others said. The presenter may share what struck him or her and what next steps might be taken as a result of the ideas generated by the discussion. *Critical friends are silent.*

AFTER THE LAST PRESENTER...

DEBRIEF (5 MIN)

The facilitator leads a conversation about the group's observation of the process. One mark of a good facilitator is his or her ability to lead a good debrief. Questions posed to the group might include: Did we have good questions? Did we stick to the questions? When was a moment when the conversations made a turn for the better? Was there any point where we went off track? Did our probing questions really push the thinking of the presenters? *Resist the urge to turn the debrief back to a discussion of the dilemma.*

TOTAL TIME: APPROXIMATELY 45 MINUTES PER PRESENTER

MAKE A "PROJECT SHEET"

The "project sheet" is a short document that sets out what's happening in the project. It's designed to be shared with student and parents. I like to keep a stack of project sheets available in my room so that anyone can quickly get up to speed on what students are doing. A typical project sheet contains the name of the project, the teachers, grade levels and content areas involved, a short project description, important learning goals, important dates, contact information, and at least one photo of what the students will do.

THE PROJECT LAUNCH

You've planned, prototyped, and tuned your project idea, and the time has come to launch the experience with your students.

The first day of the project is the launch, and it should be specifically designed to be engaging, with at least one active experience. Activities such as field work, rapid prototyping, interviews, time with community experts, and even impromptu debates offer multiple entry points and invite diverse students to share their unique perspectives and engage in innovative thinking. Furthermore, an active, engaging launch event for the project provides a shared experience to set the stage for future learning.[4]

Goals for a project launch:

- Students share a common, authentic experience that creates a context for future learning of both content and skills.

- Students understand what they will create, what they will learn and why.

- Students start to articulate their ideas about the project's essential question.

- Students create work that serves as a baseline to help peers and teachers identify strengths and areas for development.

- Students develop success criteria for the final product by studying a model (this could be the teacher's prototype, a professional example, or student work from a previous year).

- Students are excited about the project.

IDEAS FOR THE LAUNCH

Your project launch will probably have a few different components. Proven ideas for project launches are to:

GO OUTSIDE FOR FIELDWORK

Students, working in pairs, fan out into the neighborhood surrounding their school, to collect 10 artifacts that provide evidence of different forms of life in the area. Each pair of students then creates a small display on a tabletop with their collections and index cards that describe what each artifact is, where it was found, and what specific life forms can be understood to inhabit the specific area based on their documentation. Ultimately, students will create a field guide to the local flora and fauna, and they become wildlife biologists on day one.

BUILD A PROTOTYPE

On the first day of a project exploring Newtonian physics and rocket science, students are quickly arranged into small groups and are given a small cardboard tube, a specific amount of balsa wood, an exacto knife, glue, and a small model rocket engine. They are given a time limit and challenged to design and build a model rocket that will fly as high as possible, and, once they see the work of their classmates, to predict which rockets will fly the highest. Not all students have launched model rockets as children—and many may not be inherently interested in rocket science—so in order to begin this physics, math and engineering project, each student must try on the identities of rocket scientist and engineer. The shared experience of rapidly designing, prototyping, predicting and ultimately pressing the "launch" button for their own rockets provides multiple entry points for diverse students to engage in rocket science. And, it provides a clear understanding of one product that students may build in the course of the project.

SHOW MEDIA CLIPS THAT WITH RADICALLY DIFFERENT VIEWS ON THE ESSENTIAL QUESTION, AND USE THESE AS A BASIS FOR AN INITIAL DISCUSSION.

When a humanities teacher launched a project in which students wrote a play about a controversial case of police violence in the media at the time, he started by showing opinions from news commentators with wildly divergent perspectives on what was happening in real time, why it was happening, and who was to blame. He then went straight into a class discussion about what they had heard, and students were eager to share their opinions because the controversial issue activated their sense of justice.

For some teachers, the ideal media clips are not readily available. In that case, teachers can use their smart phones and computers to quickly create short videos of their own. Teachers can create a video diary, they can interview colleagues or community members, or even create a DIY video of the type of work students will do or the locations they will visit. For these, production values do not need to be high—the important part is that the teacher creates the video and shares the essential messages of the project with the class.

BRING IN GUEST SPEAKERS, OR GO TO THEM.

When a teacher launches a project in which students create podcasts to educate voters on local issues, a great way to begin in with local journalists coming to class—and it is even better if the teacher can get a commitment from local media to air the student-created podcasts. When a teacher launches a project in which students document personal histories of local veterans, an engaging first day would be to meet a veterans group at a museum or community center, and begin the conversations right away. Guest speakers and informal interviews on day one bring students face-to-face with the community members who live the reality of their school project every day, which is a powerful way for students to understand the authenticity of their work.

"BAKED-IN" EQUITY: CONSIDER I.E.P.s AS A DESIGN RESOURCE

Once you have identified the core learning in the project, you can provide a broad scope for demonstrating this learning, depending on an individual student's strengths.

One way to do this is to refer to students' Individualized Education Plans (IEPs) before planning the project. Perhaps an IEP can offer clues to designing a project that is accessible to all students. For example, if several IEPs offer extended time on tests, ask yourself if timed tests are essential to the core assessment of the project. Ask yourself how professionals would assess their work—would they use a test, and if so, does that test have a time limit? Perhaps everyone in the class would benefit from untimed tests, or tests offered on multiple days, or any other element of an IEP. Bake in equity from the start of the project design as much as possible; then you won't need to make many modifications later, and the ones you do make will feel more comfortable to the class as a whole.

Details like this may seem minor, but for a student they mean the difference between taking part in "the" project and having a different version of the project set aside for them. It feels better for everyone when all students are working on a project that was designed with all of them in mind.

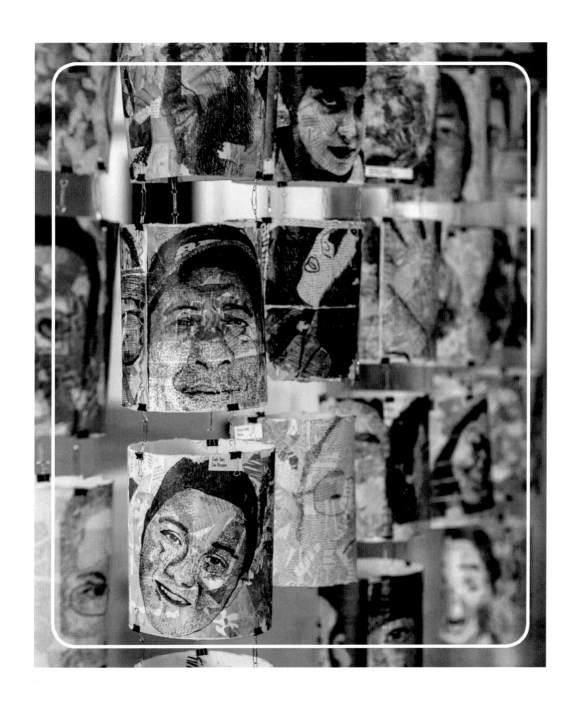

A CAVEAT ABOUT "ENGAGEMENT"

No matter how magical, meaningful, or experiential your project launch is, a portion of your students might be skeptical at the start of a project. Don't let it bring you down—it's normal.

In part, this is because some people are inclined to treat anything new with a certain amount of suspicion, and any project launch is, by definition, something new. In addition, most of the time there is no such thing as "engaging the class"—you are engaging a group of distinct individuals clustering themselves into ever-shifting groups within the class, and the very event of one group expressing enthusiasm for what's happening in class may alert another subgroup to treat it with suspicion.

And, before a project can end with students triumphantly exclaiming "I never knew I could do that!" they may have to say, "I don't know if we can do that..."

THE DREADED "WE'VE DONE THIS BEFORE"

It's a terrible moment: the teacher is in full stride describing the incredible project the class is about to embark on, when a student's hand shoots up. "We already did this two years ago," the student announces.

If you teach at a school where other teachers are doing projects, this is bound to happen. In order to minimize this, it may be smart to keep track of what teachers in the previous grade to each year—but some forms of repetition are bound to happen anyway. And, project tuning sessions are great opportunities to connect with other colleagues and ask if students have done similar work before.

Fortunately, there are good responses to the students who say "we've done this before":

When students inform you that they already did a project that, to them, sounds similar to your project, and you can hear their frustration that they're just going to be going over old ground, try something like this:

"That is great! If you have experience with this, that means we can really be professional in what we do—and we are going to need to be great, because a lot of people are waiting to see your work."

ONE MORE THING... EVEN IF YOU DON'T FEEL READY FOR THIS, YOU'RE READY!

Launching your first project is a leap into the unknown. For that matter, so is launching your 100th. You will have ups, and down, successes, and failures, and you'll go from feeling like the greatest teacher in the world to the worst, sometimes in a matter of seconds—just like any other kind of teaching!

But the only way you'll learn how to do a project is to do it, so go for it! Just make sure you do the project yourself first, and do a tuning. Seriously, you won't regret it. Good luck!

PUBLIC PRESENTATIONS OF STUDENT LEARNING—WHETHER AS OPEN HOUSES, FORMAL PRESENTATIONS, CONFERENCES, OR BY PLACING STUDENT WORK AMONG AUTHENTIC USERS—DRIVE PROJECT-DESIGN PROCESSES AND CREATE OPPORTUNITIES FOR AUTHENTIC DIALOGICAL ASSESSMENT.

CHAPTER 2

MAKING STUDENT LEARNING PUBLIC

BY KELLY WILLIAMS
HIGH TECH HIGH MEDIA ARTS

SHARE YOUR *LEARNING*

The classrooms have been transformed. Lights are dimmed in one classroom, and a student-built stage spans the space where a partition between classrooms once loomed. A spotlight shines on the center of the empty stage, and two students prepare to open the doors to let the audience in. Across the hall in a different room, black table cloths cover the tables and student-built rockets are displayed in rows, with placards showing mathematical equations and scientific diagrams. Students stand among their work, talking with adults, pointing to rocket parts to explain scientific theories and justify their engineering decisions. Outside of the classrooms, student-produced art lines the halls and there are tables set up with refreshments. On most days, these spaces are amok with sawdust, tools, art supplies, and project prototypes. Typically, students sit akimbo over chairs, tables, and stools, and whiteboards are covered in math formulas or English lessons. But this night is different. This night, the school is intentionally designed to house and display student work in a professional manner. This is Exhibition Night.

An "exhibition" is a culminating event in which students share their learning with an authentic audience. The practices of making student public takes many forms. It might consist of an open house in which the school or a venue in the community acts as a gallery where students can showcase their work and learning. Students also describe their learning to authentic audiences in formal presentations of learning, in which they reflect on their educational experiences and present a portfolio of evidence to a panel of peers and adults, who offer support and feedback. And, students share their learning in student-led conferences, which flip the well-known parent-teacher model and feature the student facilitating the discussion.

From exhibition events to formal presentations of learning to student-led conferences, project-based learning publicly situates student learning in authentic contexts. Student work is more visible and is more relevant when it is shared with a wider audience of families, communities members, experts, visitors, and peers, especially compared to a singular audience of a teacher. Engaging with the audience makes the work real, and puts students' reflections on their learning at the center of a community conversation. As a result, the stakes are raised for everyone involved. In this way, public presentations of learning, regardless of format, injects into classroom culture the expectation that everyone involved needs to share, discuss, and strive for their best work possible.

AN EXHIBITION OF LEARNING

Exhibitions of learning are more than just displays of high-quality student products, where visitors trek through and simply admire the work. They are dynamic, interactive events in which young people show the world they can contribute meaningfully to it, and they share the thinking behind their contributions. Students are the stars of this show, and their work and learning processes are meant to be reviewed, appraised, questioned, and appreciated. In doing so, students are tasked with sharing the "how" as well as what decisions went into the "doing." In this way, exhibition is an opportunity for students to display their minds' handiwork.

In many parts of school, the seeds of high quality exhibitions have already taken root. Theater and music classes regularly perform for authentic public audiences, for example, while art, multimedia, and journalism classes regularly display their products in various forums and media. Engineering classes and sports teams attend competitions, where they put their skills on display and actively test what they have learned. In project-based learning, all classes bring their work to the world in a similar fashion, and take it one step further by also describing their learning—that is, explaining what went into the creation and display of a meaningful final product.

Imagine a theater performance in which the audience mingles in a lobby adorned with student-created schematics of the set design and lighting, original blueprints of the costumes and props, and critiqued drafts, prototypes, and scale models of each. Imagine that the play's program was student created, and includes student reflections about the process of key elements of the overall project. Picture students mingling with the audience, wearing nametags that say, "Ask me about the physics of stage lighting," or "Ask me about the narrative arc of my script." In such a scene, the play is but one piece of work on display, and the audience is invited into a larger conversation about how it was made, what the students learned, and how this impacts their lives moving forward.

QUESTIONS TO ADDRESS FOR A SUCCESSFUL EXHIBITION INCLUDE:

- HOW will we exhibit our work including artifacts of the process?
- WHERE will we exhibit our work? Why there?
- HOW will we schedule the exhibition event?
- WHO is involved and WHAT is their role?
- WHAT comes after the exhibition event—how will the products and processes live on?

LESSONS FROM ANDERSON VALLEY HIGH SCHOOL'S FIRST EXHIBITIONS

DAVID BALLANTINE, INDUSTRIAL DESIGN
KIM JENDERSECK, SCIENCE
MITCH MENDOSA, ENGLISH AND VIDEO PRODUCTION
DONNA PIERSON-PUGH, GRANT ADMINISTRATOR
JIM SNYDER, MATH AND MUSIC PRODUCTION

Jim Snyder, Donna Pierson-Pugh, Mitch Mendosa, David Ballantine, and Kim Jenderseck are leading a grassroots revolution in Anderson Valley, CA, by leveraging the power of exhibitions to bring about student ownership of learning experiences, other teachers trying PBL practices, and parents seeing their students' experiences at school more authentically.

COLLABORATE WITH A COLLEAGUE

Building a team, or even finding a single partner, provides structural and emotional support and the new ideas needed to create an exhibition. The job of facilitating a public exhibition of student learning involves lots of small tasks and it can be overwhelming—having a partner to share this work transforms a potentially intimidating job into a challenging and exciting project.

GO FOR IT, AND LEARN BY DOING

The Anderson Valley team committed themselves to more than one exhibition so they could learn from experience and quickly bring others on board.

HTH co-founder Rob Riordan advises teachers to "Just do it. Hold it in the evening, when colleagues and community can attend. Invite everyone you can think of— the mayor, school board, city council, parents, local university folks, etc."

Many schools already have experts in events similar to exhibitions of learning. Gather ideas from the school newspaper or yearbook, the theater or orchestra, sports teams, science fairs, or anyone who has participated in similar events. Find the ideas you like the best, give them a try, and set aside time to learn from your experience. Set a date and go for it!

MAKE IT PUBLIC

Exhibitions of learning need an audience. Set a date (this may be the most important step), choose a location, and share this information with students, families, and colleagues. As the date gets closer, create a poster and an online marketing campaign. This can be as simple as a poster placed around campus along with emails to the school community, or far more complex; take ideas from marketing that you appreciate in your community, such as movie releases, non-profit campaigns, or anything similar.

MAKE STUDENTS CO-DESIGNERS

Students have valuable ideas about the design of important aspects of the event, from how to spread the word in the community to how the audience should experience their work. Teachers are wise to leverage their energy, ideas, and expertise—students that co-design exhibitions of learning are inherently invested. In Anderson Valley, students who participated in the first exhibition collected their thoughts, created plans for the next one, formed committees to implement their ideas, and supported teachers new to the process. The Anderson Valley teachers noted that these students invited their friends—and after the exhibition, teachers noted in a staff survey how powerful it was to see students presenting their learning to other students in an authentic context.

BRING PBL TO THE CORE WITH EXHIBITION

When a showcase event like an exhibition of student learning is on the calendar, teachers and students naturally design, critique, and revise their work to prepare it for the public. Importantly, the Anderson Valley team noted the positive changes in learning and engagement when students and teachers directed their energy towards sharing their learning with an authentic audience from their community.

HOW TO EXHIBIT WORK AND LEARNING

When embarking on a project's design, teachers and students should discuss and plan how they will exhibit not just the final work, but also how they can preserve artifacts of the process so as to demonstrate learning. Will the final product be a physical object, a performance, the results of research, an interactive experience, or a service? And what drawings, drafts, sketches, prototypes, interviews, brainstorming output, preliminary data, critical feedback, or other items will be created along the way that can be displayed to exhibit the learning process?

Generally, an exhibition event is structured along a spectrum. On one side is performance; on the other, curation of products. These qualities are not mutually exclusive, and elements from one side of the spectrum are typically brought over to support the other (consider the example of a theater project described above).

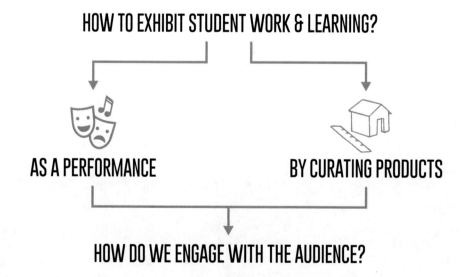

Whether the exhibition of learning is primarily a theatrically-styled performance or a gallery-style showcase, elements of each are brought together to address two questions:

- How do students meaningfully engage with their audience?
- How do students share not just the end result of the project, and not just the specific steps they took to get there, but their learning?

For example, students who showcase documentary films in a theater can:

Curate artifacts such as:

- Storyboards, drafts, or photographs that indicate learning processes.
- Scientific data and maps.
- The equipment used to produce their films.

Interact with the audience by:

- Facilitating question-and-answer panels about their learning processes.
- Wearing name tags before and after the screenings with prompts of what to discuss.
- Doing hands-on, interactive demonstrations of how to use technical equipment.

Students who curate a gallery of student-built robots can:

Create the dynamic nature and energy of a performance by:

- Demonstrating what each robot can do.
- Presenting the science behind robot creation and the ethics of using them in society.
- Showing, narrating and discussing films and slideshows of students' working processes in the classroom.

Interact with the audience by:

- Hosting panel discussions and question-and-answer sessions.
- Walking guests through the process of how to design/build specific parts of a robot.
- Displaying a conversational prompt with each robot that helps students and guests begin a conversation.

Curating work is vital to demonstrating its underlying learning and rigor. Curation is an artform in itself and teachers should look to professional models like museums, art galleries, and stores for inspiration.

Teachers should think about how to transform space to best display products and processes in an aesthetically pleasing and compelling way. Teachers should also consider how traffic will flow through the space. This depends on the space, the project, and the student, and teachers' design preferences. Elements that consistently work no matter the project include displaying an overall project description for visitors to read and generally transforming the space from a classroom to site of a public exhibition.

Ideas for curating the exhibition space include:

- Install a process wall or display case full of student work like prototypes, drafts, and photos that visitors see as they enter the space or as they move through the exhibition.

- Play a process video that loops on a screen in the exhibition space.

- Cover tables with black cloths and bring in special lighting to focus guests' attention on students and their work.

- Hang posters with descriptions of work samples and process by fishing line from the ceiling over a display table of artifacts.

- Set up stations that feature laptops and headphones, where audience members can experience multimedia products.

WHERE TO EXHIBIT STUDENT LEARNING

Artifacts of student learning, including final products, should have a place to live after the project ends; work should be displayed in the style of professionals either in the school's hallway, at the local library, or at a local business. Making student work a semi-permanent component of the school environment or local community shows students their work matters.

Questions to consider:

- Will the exhibition take place on campus, such as in a classroom, auditorium, or gym?
- Will it take place off campus, such as in a museum, local business, art studio, or community center?
- Will the exhibition be during the day, the evening, a school night, or over a weekend?
- Is the event intended to be one time only, or will the work be displayed semi-permanently?

On-site or open-house exhibitions display products and processes for audiences who gather in the school space. These exhibitions may include plays and performances suited for the school's stage or auditorium, or feature exhibits that invite community members and parents to interact with students and their work. This type of curation helps to build community and school culture.

Off-site exhibitions display student work outside of the school—at a coffee shop, in a business's lobby, at a local nonprofit organization, etc. The space should have an authentic connection to the project. These locales may be where the work will be used or where those who requested the high-quality final product work, live, or act. Curating student endeavors is in professional spaces brings authenticity to classroom work.

TRANSFORMATION EXHIBITION
S.O.A.R. ACADEMY
EAST MESA, SAN DIEGO, CA

ERICA PALICKI, MATH & SCIENCE
SAMANTHA HOWERTON, HUMANITIES
DOROTHY CORONA, SPECIAL EDUCATION

"IF IT CAN BE DONE IN OUR ENVIRONMENT, IT CAN BE DONE ANYWHERE."
—*Samantha Howerton*

Teachers at this juvenile hall-based school use project-based learning to teach their transient student population character-education based on a particular theme. For the theme of transformation, teachers had the students—who ranged in age from 13 to 19—create work during their two-hour block classes. The audience at exhibition consisted of classroom teachers, counselors, administrators, probation officers, visiting officers, and medical staff. Because this facility houses youth who have histories and records that typically include violence, it can be hard to authorize visitors to attend exhibition. Teachers and students therefore exhibited work in their individual classrooms in lieu of an open common space for an outside audience.

Approximately 120 students displayed work for the Transformation Exhibition; only about 30 students lived in the facility on the day of the exhibition event. This demonstrates an ongoing challenge for these teachers: the school's high turnover rate. Some students are only there for only 24 hours, but teachers have even these students complete a component of the project to exhibit.

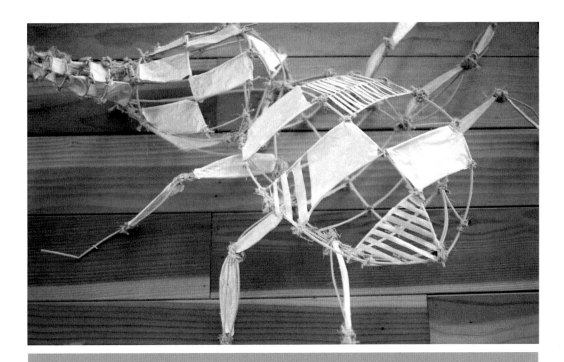

Products on Display:

- Autobiographies
- Transformation Plans
- A Call to Action
- "I am..." Poem
- Abstract Art that shows the "before and after" of the youths' lives

After exhibition, students reflected positively on the experience. They enjoyed hearing visitors offer feedback, praise, and acknowledge their work. They felt proud of their work, they appreciated the display of their peers' work, and many students asked teachers if they could call home—a rarity—and share the work, learning, and growth they had experienced with their families.

Potential off-site exhibition locations include:

- coffee shops or restaurants
- the public library
- a nature center
- a public park or building
- an office building
- a nonprofit organization
- a museum
- an art gallery
- City Hall
- a performance space such as a theater or concert venue
- a university building

HOW TO SCHEDULE AN EXHIBITION OF LEARNING

Schools may set a school-wide date for an exhibition event, or educators may determine their own dates. Once a date is established, teachers and students can plan backwards to organize curriculum and logistics. Remember to leave time after exhibition for reflection and for students to curate specific artifacts in their portfolios. Planning for exhibition can start on the first day of the semester or school year.

Questions to consider when scheduling exhibition:

- Will the exhibition event take place towards the end of the school year? Towards the end of each semester or trimester? At another date or key point in the year?
- Will the exhibition be a school-wide event? A grade-level event? A single teacher event?
- What other school-wide or community events are happening that might affect the exhibition?

- Will the exhibition take place during the day? At night? Both?
- Will the exhibition take place at school? Off-site? Both? How does this impact scheduling?
- How much time should I leave after the exhibition for reflection, portfolio development, or other classroom practices?

Communicate details about the event to students, families, professionals, and community members well in advance of exhibition. Once set, make sure the date is included on the class calendar, on the syllabus, and on project materials. As the date nears, delegate students to create an exhibition program or flyer with details like the time, location, and what to expect. Send it home to families and post it within and around the school community.

WHO IS INVOLVED AND WHAT IS THEIR ROLE

There are many moving parts to an exhibition, which can make it tricky to pull off. The task is made simpler by focusing on the roles of those responsible for the exhibition, which include the teacher, the students, and the audience.

ROLE OF THE TEACHER

The teacher understands the vision of the exhibition and its logistics. As such, he or she delegates responsibilities to students, parents, and staff.

To facilitate an authentic, successful exhibition, teachers address questions such as:

How does this exhibition event demonstrate the knowledge and skills students have learned over the course of the semester or year?

- During exhibition, students show and reflect on their projects to reveal evidence of knowledge and learning. A well-curated process and high-quality final products demonstrate the rigor and depth of student understanding.

How will I ensure that all students are deeply involved?

- Inclusive, equitable exhibitions send the message that all students—not just a select group—are capable of producing high-quality work, and will share their experiences with authentic audiences beyond the classroom.

How will I include student voice and choice in the exhibition event?

- Facilitate student participation in decisions made regarding both their work and the final exhibition presentation, and have students share these decision making process at the exhibition event.

How will I provide multiple opportunities for students to practice what they will exhibit?

- Student rehearsal deepens understanding and familiarity with expectations, as well as how they will manage exhibition logistics, deliver content, and demonstrate their skills.

How will I guide students as they create high-quality work to publicly exhibit?

- Do the project yourself first; this will help develop the project criteria and description, the scaffolds, the prototypes and final models, and rubrics that will best support high-quality student work.

How will I provide opportunities throughout the project for reflection (personal, academic, and social)?

- Providing reflective opportunities refines student thinking about learning they will share as part of their exhibition.

How and when will I communicate with students, families, community members, and professionals about exhibition?

- Early communication ensures attendance from family and community members and helps students understand the importance of a high-quality finished product and exhibition.

What structures will I put in place to help the audience interact with students at exhibition?

- Plan for meaningful audience participation and understanding via Q&A sessions, exhibition guide questions, role play expectations, and post-exhibition debriefs.

ROLE OF THE STUDENT

In many ways, the students are the products on display at exhibition. They have created beautiful, meaningful final products and displayed artifacts from rigorous processes; yet the audience comes to see the students, specifically, and to understand their experiences and growth. As a result, teachers should feature students in as many roles as possible, including promoting the event, greeting visitors, curating the work, leading presentations, interacting with participants, documenting the event, and cleaning up.

Students prepare for exhibition throughout their project, including when they critique the work of their peers and revise and reflect on their own work. These experiences teach them how to articulate their thoughts about specific elements of project work. Students practice exhibition presentation techniques in front of classmates or other grade levels. For example, a ninth grade class might invite an eleventh grade class to critique their exhibition presentations prior to the actual event to practice and receive feedback from upperclassmen who have been through the process. Overall, the role of the student is to learn—and then to share their learning.

HOW WILL I ORGANIZE MY STUDENTS TO HELP PREPARE FOR EXHIBITION?

Potential student roles prior to an exhibition of learning:

 Marketing

Design and implement a plan—and the products needed—to bring an authentic audience to the exhibition event.

Location & Floorplan

Design and implement a plan to exhibit the work. Collaborate with Curators to address questions of how student work, presentations, and students themselves are organized on the night of exhibition.

How will guests know where to enter, how to move through the experience, and where to gather?

Program

Create a professionally styled brochure, handbill, or map of the exhibition, including the title of the project, classes participating, locations of student work, and important explanatory text that helps orient visitors to the experience.

Base work off of examples from museums, tourist attractions, galleries, or parks that use such documents to help guests make the most of their experience.

Nametags

Design a simple name tag that invites interaction between the audience and the students.

Name tags likely include the individual's name, the name of the project, and relevant and engaging topics or questions to discuss.

Curation

Collaborate with the Location & Floorplan team to design and implement a plan to thoughtfully display student work in the venue during the exhibition event.

Ensure that all work samples from all students are displayed elegantly and highly professionally.

Collaborate with the teachers to organize materials, instruction, and support needed to curate student work well.

Technology

Arrange for computers, projectors, audio support, and related technology to function seamlessly at the exhibition event.

Ensure that all student work meets tech specs.

WHAT WILL EACH STUDENT DO DURING EXHIBITION?

Teachers should organize expectations, responsibilities, and a schedule for students. Address questions such as when students should arrive, how long they are expected to be at exhibition, what they should wear, and what they will do during the event.

Potential student roles during an exhibition of learning include:

Greeters
Welcome guests and orient them to the experience, distribute the exhibition program, and manage related work.

Tech Crew
Supports and maintains projectors, audio equipment, cameras, lighting, etc.

Documentarians
Ensure that all students, their work, and the overall experience is photographed and videoed for later reflections, sharing online, continued exhibition, and portfolios.

Presentation Coaches
Students coach their peers to thoughtfully present their work, give keynote talks, and share their learning.

Learners
Ultimately, all students hold this role. Address goals of how students will engage with each other about their work during the event, and how students will learn about other products or projects on display.

WHAT WILL EACH STUDENT DO AFTER EXHIBITION?

Potential student roles after an exhibition of learning:

 Curation & Living Projects

Create and implement and plan to semi-permanently display student work in school—or other locations—beyond exhibition.

Address specific concerns regarding the potential need to change, repair or move anything to curate the work well in school after the event.

Ensures that students, teachers, families and members of the broader community continue to have appropriate levels of access to the work.

Answers questions regarding how broadly the work will be shared beyond exhibition.

 Documentation

Ensures that photography and video content are widely shared for later reflections, online curation, continued exhibition, and portfolios.

 Reflection

Guides peers and teachers through a process of looking back on experiences, asking questions, and fostering thoughtful, deliberate practice moving forward.[1]

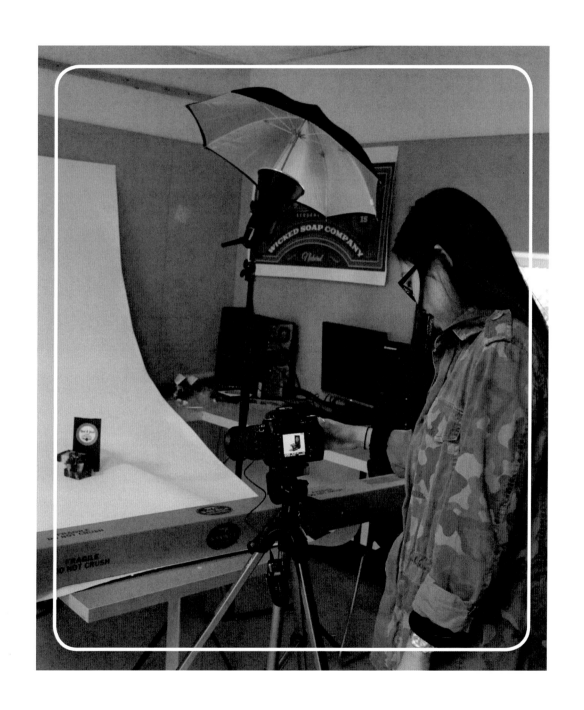

ROLE OF THE AUDIENCE

An exhibition's audience might include family members, community members, peers, educators, school administrators, agency representatives, professionals, and other stakeholders and interested parties. Student motivation and engagement increase when their work is increasingly important to an authentic audience; exhibition is enriched when the exhibition audience meaningfully participates in the experience, and their participation should not be an afterthought. To manage this task, elicit help from parents to help plan, set up, organize, delegate tasks, and help with transportation if the exhibition is off-site.

Memorable exhibitions often hinge on meaningful interactions with an authentic audience. Potential audience roles include:

- Observe students and interview them about their work and learning.
- Assess student work and and offer feedback.
- Interact with exhibitors through role play exercises, Q&A, and informal critique.
- Serve as panelists.
- Participate in simulations.
- Display or use student work on location.
- Act on reports to make policy take action.
- Receive services or use products from students.

Teachers can help audiences understand their role at exhibition by curating a well-formatted experience; a solid structure helps all participants interact with each other more effectively. Teachers and students might also circulate a brochure that explains how audience members can interact with students, a checklist to guide audience members through the experience, specific questions audience members might ask students about their work, and a feedback questionnaire that can be filled out at each station or turned in at the end of the event.

WHAT COMES AFTER EXHIBITION?

After exhibition, facilitate reflective exercises (written and conversational) to help students process the experience, celebrate their successes, and connect the many purposes of sharing their learning with the broader community. Teachers use practices such as journaling, think-pair-share prompts, critique sessions, or class-wide discussions. All student perspectives should be explored in a safe environment.

TAKE-AWAYS

- Exhibition should not be tacked on to the end of a project—it should be the culminating piece of an extensive, iterative project that featured critique and revision to determine both the project's steps and quality of student work.

- Build in time for meaningful reflection (and helpful clean-up!) after exhibition. Avoid scheduling it for the very last day or night of the year/semester.

- Teachers should do the project themselves in advance to set up design elements and get insight into the project's more difficult components. This will also help teachers know how to curate the exhibition.

- All student work can be celebrated and all students should be included in exhibitions of learning.

- While exhibitions are very much centered around student process and production, teachers must organize, plan in advance, set expectations, and delegate tasks to students and the audience.

- Exhibitions are powerful agents of school change.

Overall, the visibility and transparency inherent in an exhibition is part of its magic. Both students and teachers can use the experience to further improve their practice. Teachers can work to build upon exhibitions of work that they see among colleagues and in the world beyond school. Students can check in with their peers through the critique process to do the same, and push themselves higher. Inevitably, students internalize what defines quality work, and learn to assess themselves to determine whether they meet the standards they set. The power of exhibition to evoke school change lies in the rise of meaningful activity both inside and outside the classroom, as it results in a faculty and student body more focused on curriculum reform and community involvement.

PRESENTATIONS OF LEARNING

Imagine a classroom that is arranged so a table with several chairs behind it faces a projector screen. Teachers, students, and community members sit at this table like members of a board or a panel. One student dressed in professional attire stands in front of them with her back to the screen, which projects a slideshow of evidence from her collection of work from the last semester. There is an infographic and a journalism article about diabetes research (created in humanities and biology classes), accompanied by a statistical analysis of diabetes data (done in math class). The student discusses herself as a learner, reflects deeply on her work, thinks critically about her academic progress and her social-emotional growth, and answers questions from the panel of adults and peers. This presentation is a year-end rite of passage in which the student advocates for why she should advance to the next grade level.

Presentations of learning (POLs) are a rite of passage at the end of a semester or school year in which students describe their learning, supported by artifacts and evidence selected from a portfolio of their work from class, to a panel of peers and adults who ask questions, offer feedback, and provide support.[2] POLs build specific skills in students, including the ability to reflect honestly and deeply about one's identity as a learner, set goals and assess progress, formally present to a variety of audiences, ground personal arguments in evidence, and build a growth mindset.

Logistically, POLs may feature a single presenter in front of a panel or take the format of a Socratic seminar. The framework depends on grade level and the needs of teachers and students.

Importantly, all students complete presentations of learning. This ensures that all students have a chance to reflect on what they have learned, plan their next steps, and ask for guidance in doing so. POLs make it impossible for a student to fall through the cracks; they provide an opportunity for all students to be seen and heard. Finally, POLs offer a window into what students find most interesting, meaningful, and important about their educational experiences.

QUESTIONS TO ADDRESS FOR CONDUCTING SUCCESSFUL PRESENTATIONS OF LEARNING INCLUDE:

- HOW should we structure POLs?
- WHERE should we do POLs?
- HOW will we schedule POLs?
- WHO is involved in the POL and WHAT is their role?
- WHAT next?

HOW TO DO POLs

POLs can be done in multiple ways that depend on the grade level, the experience, and the teacher. The nature of POLs vary; some are transitional POLs in which students show their readiness to move on to the next grade level; others are internship POLs in which students share what they have done and learned over the course of an internship experience; still others are mid-year semester POLs, in which students discuss their experiences over several months and articulate learning goals for the upcoming semester. Each type necessitates a portfolio of work that students can use as evidence to support their growth.

- Conducting a successful POL involves providing students with the following:
- POL expectations and rubric
- Models of POLs to critique and discuss as a class
- Scaffolds and time in class to prepare for POLs
- POL practice and critique sessions—peer critique, advisory critique, whole class critique
- Time to reflect after the POL

POLs are traditionally done at the end of a semester, mid-year, or any other point at which it is pertinent to discuss learning goals. Variations on POLs include the Internship Presentation of Learning (iPOL), which is done upon completing an internship experience, and the Transitional Presentation of Learning (tPOL), done at the end of a school year or at a transitional point between schools as a way to show readiness to advance to the next grade or educational level.

WHERE TO DO POLs

The location of the POL is usually dictated by its content. For example, students may be required to do their internship POL at their internship site. This gives the presentation authenticity, makes it easier for the student's internship mentor and other colleagues to attend, and allows the student's teacher and younger classmates to experience the workplace environment. Other POLs take place in the school; younger students can be introduced to the practice in the safety of their classrooms, while more experienced students can present in their classrooms or a more public space, and POL panels can be populated with members of the school community.

HOW TO SCHEDULE POLs

It is important to communicate about the details regarding a high-stakes event like a POL well in advance. Many school sites determine a day, week, or schedule for POLs early in the year, and let parents know right away. However, it is also important that teachers communicate with students, families, and community members about the event as it nears. One possible schedule would be to have a new POL begin every 20 minutes; assign students to groups and rooms so that they know where to be and when to report there.

Questions to address when scheduling POLs:

- How frequently will POLs take place? At the end of each semester or trimester? At the end of the school year for every grade? Or, just for those moving from elementary to middle, middle to high school, or graduating high school?

- How long should each POL be?

- Will POLs be a school-wide event?
- What other school-wide and/or community events are happening that might affect POLs?
- Will POLs take place during the day? After school?
- Will POLs take place in a specific class? Advisory? Across grade levels or teaching teams?
- Will POLs take place on-site or off-site?

WHO IS INVOLVED IN THE POL AND WHAT IS THEIR ROLE?

Teachers must establish roles for themselves, their students, and the audience or panel, which will likely include other students, teachers, family members, and community members.

ROLE OF THE TEACHER

The teacher understands the purpose of the POL and its logistics, and thus organizes students, other teachers, family members, and community members accordingly.

To facilitate a meaningful POL, teachers address the following questions:
- What are the requirements of the POL?
- How will students select and organize their work?
- How will we assess each POL?

As teachers establish POL requirements, they address the following questions:
- What is the structure of the POL?
- What protocols will be followed?
- How long will each POL last?
- What attire is required?

To support students in crafting a portfolio of work samples for their POLs, address the following:

- How will students use their collections of work as evidence for their reflections about their learning?

- How should students choose work samples for their POL?

- How should students share work samples with their audience at their POLs?

- Is the collection of work digital or is it a physical product?

In determining assessment criteria, teachers address the following questions:

- What do we seek to understand about each student's performance?

- Will we use a checklist, rubric, or other template for feedback?

- Who will provide feedback on each student's presentation?

- Do students have a chance to revise or deliver another presentation if they receive substantial critical feedback?

Naturally, the answers to all of the above questions vary, depending on the context: teacher and student experience with similar presentations, grade level, and more. To help students prepare for their POLs, teachers:

- Let students practice presentations in small groups or to the whole class.

- Bring in older students to mentor younger ones.

- Provide opportunities to analyze examples of past POLs and similar professional speeches.

- Supply sentence starters ("I chose this artifact because it is a good example of my growth in...").

- Give students clear expectations and guidelines for how they will be assessed.

- Offer guidelines regarding posture, tone, volume, eye contact, pace, etc..

ROLE OF THE STUDENT

Successful POLs hinge on students feeling ownership over the presentation's narrative and the specific work that is highlighted. Students should personalize their presentation to highlight insights and experiences relevant to their goals, rather than being required to include specific samples or content from class. Above all, students should reflect on academic learning and character development and share personal successes, challenges, and next steps.

The following prompts should be posed to help students organize their presentations and collections of evidence (in fact, these questions can be used as the structure to guide each POL):[3]

- What is the most meaningful work I have done this year/semester, and why?
- How have I been successful in school/this class?
- What challenges have I faced in school/this class?
- How am I doing as an individual student in school/this class?
- How am I doing as a member of this community?

ROLE OF THE AUDIENCE

A POL's audience might consist of parents, advisors, former teachers, community members, extended family members, other students, professionals, and school administrators. It is important for the teacher to think about what kind of panel will be best for making students feel challenged yet supported. For example, ninth grade panels might consist of parents, other students, and an advisor, while seniors would benefit from having community members, family members, and a variety of students in attendance. Teachers should be aware that the stakes are increased when they make a panel less familiar and more formal. Thus, teachers must be mindful and intentional when establishing the composition of POL panels .

Once the panel is established, teachers should provide explicit instructions. They might hand out a formal agenda with potential questions to ask; they might write directions on the board; or might give verbal instructions before each POL begins.

WHAT NEXT?

It is critical and necessary to engage in thoughtful, deliberate reflection after any significant event like a POL. To this end, students should be given the space to reflect on their POL, either in writing or verbally. This allows students to improve their presentation skills, heighten reflective practices, and sets them up to do even better at future presentations. Younger students may view POLs as terrifying, but as they get older and complete more, public presentations become less daunting; students understand them to be a meaningful part of their education.

Take-aways

- Students are required to make key decisions regarding what to include in their POL based on clear expectations.

- POLs empower students to understand themselves as learners and to advocate for themselves.

- POLs give students a choice in presentation and the opportunity to share points of view.

- POLs give students the opportunity to synthesize their learning and reflect on their progress.

Overall, POLs have a lasting effect on the school and classroom community. These evidence-based inquiries reflect back onto classroom practice, allowing for improvement and perhaps even school-wide change. The presentations become part of the school's fabric, as students take ownership of their growth at various levels in their education and teachers hear their students' voices and affect change in their classroom as a result.

STUDENT-LED CONFERENCES

It's mid-semester. A student, his teacher, and a family member sit around a table. The student's laptop is open to his digital portfolio as he discusses his progress thus far in the semester. He celebrates a personal narrative he wrote for English class by pointing out his use of voice and reflects on how and why he is struggling with a particular project. He sets goals for the rest of the semester and establishes a plan for how to achieve these. The student is the leader in this discussion: this is his student-led conference (SLC).

Traditional parent-teacher conferences often only passively include the student, if at all. Student-led conferences are just the opposite. In SLCs, students lead family members and teachers in a reflective conversation about their progress grounded in artifacts and evidence from class. The discussion goes beyond merely showing assignments. Instead, it is a deeper conversation about areas of strength and growth as identified by the student, and draws on specific pieces of work selected by the student as evidence of his or her experiences in school. Traditionally, parent-teacher conferences are reserved for younger students or for those who are struggling in school. SLCs are for all students, as every student needs the opportunity to open windows into his or her learning experiences and lead a thoughtful conversation with important adults who will provide support for progress and growth.

SLCs are a vital way to empower students to take an active role in their learning and to communicate their experience and plans for the future to their family members and teachers. SLCs provide an opportunity for students to build personal agency and develop confidence in their academics and communication skills. In conducting SLCs, students also develop skills that will be vital as they progress through school and beyond. Like exhibition and POLs, students learn how to organize and present information, make a claim and support it with evidence, ask and answer questions, adapt their speech to the appropriate setting, make appropriate eye contact, and reflect and assess their strengths, challenges, and goals. SLCs function as a student-engaged assessment piece where students are able to make connections between their attitude, effort, practice, and increased achievement. They offer a way for students to develop a growth mindset and are an ideal way for students to demonstrate their learning to others.

SLCs invite families into an important conversation about learning. They bridge gaps between school and home by helping families understand the school's values and what their student's learning process looks like. Learning becomes transparent as parents are invited into the conversation with their son or daughter and the teacher contributes supportive dialogue.

QUESTIONS TO ADDRESS FOR SUCCESSFUL STUDENT-LED CONFERENCES INCLUDE:

- HOW will we structure SLCs?
- WHERE should we hold SLCs?
- HOW will we schedule SLCs?
- WHO is involved in the SLC and WHAT is their role?
- WHAT next?

HOW TO STRUCTURE SLCS

There are many ways to do SLCs and it is dependent upon teacher preference, grade level, school calendar, family needs, and available time. It is important that SLCs occur midway through the grading period or sooner to provide feedback the student can work with; students should have enough time to make adjustments and improvements before report cards are issued. Timing will help establish the agenda of the SLC and its implementation structure.

Potential structures for SLCs include:

Individual SLC with all teachers.

Strengths: all teachers are present and informed, family member connects with all teachers.

Challenges: time consuming.

Individual SLC with one teacher that represents a teaching team or grade level.

Strengths: allows for a longer, more in-depth conference because SLCs are divided among a teaching team.

Challenges: teacher is responsible for disseminating information to other teachers; families do not meet with every teacher.

Individual SLC with advisor or homeroom teacher.

Strengths: advisor is consistent in student's school life and can speak to their growth.

Challenges: teachers are not directly involved and informed; families do not meet with every teacher.

Multiple SLCs take place in one area and all teachers rotate in and out of each.

Strengths: efficient use of time, student takes ownership over conference, as it is primarily between students and their families, with teachers cycling in or out as needed.

Challenges: teachers could potentially miss meeting with all students and families.

WHERE TO DO SLCs

Students and family members should learn where SLCs are taking place: in a classroom, conference room, offices, the school library, common areas in a grade level, etc. Teachers should consider comfort level, noise level, and the arrangement of the room itself. Most SLCs will take place in the classroom, but other spaces like a teacher's office or a conference room may be used as well.

HOW TO SCHEDULE SLCs

It is essential that the SLC schedule is set up well in advance, similar to scheduling POLs, and that families understand the significance of SLCs and what to expect. It is also important that SLCs be scheduled for times and places that allow for the greatest turnout. Teachers should make appointments that accommodate parents' schedules, have translators available if necessary, and make backup plans should parents be unavailable.

Questions to consider when scheduling SLCs include:

- When will SLCs take place?
- Will SLCs be conducted as a teaching team? As a single teacher event?
- What other school-wide and/or community events are happening that might affect SLCs?
- Will SLCs take place during the day? At night?
- Where will SLCs take place?

Ways to schedule SLCs:

- Send a letter/mail home that includes pre-filled SLC time slots and the option to change as necessary.
- Directly call home to speak with a family member about scheduling (older students can call or email parents during class or otherwise be expected to assist in the process).
- Send a letter/email home that includes a way for families to sign up for a time slot, i.e. SignUp Genius, Google Calendar, or other online sign-up platform.
- Students call parent/guardian in class to schedule the SLC.

If parents are unable to attend the SLC:

- Video or record the conference with a teacher to share with parents.
- Invite another family member, school administrator, counselor, or advisor to step in.
- Document the student's SLC goals and discussion to share with parents.

WHO IS INVOLVED IN THE SLC AND WHAT IS THEIR ROLE?

It is important for teachers, students, and audience members to clearly understand their roles at a student-led conference. SLCs work best when teachers and parents take a step back and students take charge.

SAMPLE LETTER TO FAMILIES ABOUT SLCs IN ENGLISH:

Greetings Parents & Guardians,

Welcome to Student Led Conference season for the Spring 2017 semester. Student Led Conferences, or SLCs, are a great opportunity to come to school to see your student's work and talk about progress and goals for the semester and beyond.

The SLC schedule is attached to this email and available on our digital portfolio. The schedule can be altered to suit your needs.

We have set aside Wednesday and Thursday afternoon for families who prefer to come to school in the later afternoon or early evening. Earlier times on Thursday are reserved for those who need an early afternoon SLC time.

If your time does not work for you and your family, please contact _____with one or two other time slots as suggestions. Please note that we cannot accommodate more than four families per fifteen-minute time slot.

You can reach us at _____

We look forward to seeing you in a couple weeks!

Saludos Padres y Tutores,

Bienvenidos a la temporada de conferencias dirigidas por los estudiantes (SLCs) para el semestre de primavera del 2017. Las conferencias dirigidas por los estudiantes son una gran oportunidad para venir a la escuela a ver el trabajo de su estudiante y hablar sobre su progreso y sus metas para el semestre y más allá.

El calendario de SLC se adjunta a este correo electrónico y está disponible en nuestro portafolip digital (DP). El horario puede ser modificado para satisfacer sus necesidades.

Hemos reservado el miércoles y el jueves por la tarde para las familias que prefieren venir a la escuela un poco más tarde. Las horas más tempranas del jueves están reservadas para aquellos que necesitan una hora de SLC más temprana.

Si la hora asignada no funciona para usted y su familia, por favor comuníquese con _____ con una o dos horas sugeridas en las cuales estan disponibles. Tenga en cuenta que no podemos acomodar a más de cuatro familias por intervalo de tiempo de quince minutos.

Puede comunicarse con nosotros en _____

Esperamos verlos en un par de semanas!

THE ROLE OF THE TEACHER

In addition to communicating the importance of SLCs and developing the schedule, teachers must work with students regarding their commitment to academic success. A teacher must establish clear expectations and guidelines for students, arrange time for student reflection, provide SLC guiding questions, and supply a space for SLC practice. Throughout all of these activities, teachers facilitate student leadership over the SLC with a few key practices.

How will I prepare my students for SLCs?

- Provide clear expectations and guidelines.
- Help students understand and practice their role.
- Provide time for students to prepare for SLCs.
- Help students select work, prepare reflections, and practice presentation skills.
- Provide SLC sentence starters/scripts for students.
- Help students learn how to look at and reflect on work through simulations and critique sessions.
- Watch or simulate an SLC with students and discuss/critique (especially helpful for younger students).

What will students share during the SLC?

- Process and products in student portfolios
- Reflections and feedback in student portfolios
- Growth using evidence
- Strengths and areas of weakness using evidence
- Specific and attainable (yet challenging) goals

THE ROLE OF THE STUDENT

Students are the leaders, presenters, and facilitators in a meaningful student-led conference. They have arrived at the conference with a collection of artifacts that illustrate their experiences in school, and they understand the need to speak to various questions about their education and guide a conversation with at least two important stakeholders in their lives: their teacher and a parent or guardian.

With teacher assistance, students select work they are proud of and articulate how the sample provides evidence of their progress toward specific learning goals or skills. Prior to the SLC, students practice with a peer so they are ready to lead the conversation. At the SLC, students answer open-ended questions about specific experiences in school or follow a protocol to ensure a conversation with appropriate depth and breadth. The questions, collection of work, and rehearsals provide students with the framework to lead an important conversation about their learning.[4]

The student is in charge. The structure of the SLC helps empower students and builds a sense of responsibility and accountability for their own learning. It shows students that they can talk to their parents about their learning, and gives them a framework for doing so. The student is expected to present his/her learning in detail and depth. They should not merely describe assignments completed in class, but rather reflect on personal growth and explain what was deeply learned through that work. The student can use the SLC to help teachers and parents understand what helps him or her learn, as well as what makes learning challenging. Finally, the SLC should be viewed as a communication tool. It is an opportunity for students to voice their needs, for teachers and families to help set up supports, and for everyone to celebrate accomplishments and growth.

SLCs help students:

- Make key decisions about what work to share and why, using the work as evidence.
- See themselves as learners.
- Learn to advocate for themselves.
- Practice having reflective conversations about themselves as learners.
- Build presentations skills.

THE ROLE OF THE AUDIENCE

SLC audience members are typically family members and/or guardians. The audience member's role is to be present, listen carefully to the student's presentation, ask thoughtful questions, and support the student's learning goals and academic progress. SLCs place family members in an authentic, helpful role. The teacher should provide an opportunity for audience members to offer reflections and questions as a means of extending dialogue. SLCs can go awry should family members become fixated on low grades or uncompleted work, especially if the SLC lacks a safe space and structure to discuss supports and strategies for moving forward. Teachers can intentionally plan for this potential pitfall by providing family members with tools such as clear protocols for dilemmas (this may even be the opportunity to have a private conversation later), and supportive yet probing questions to ask of the student. These tools can be emailed home or provided directly to families at the SLC in the form of a pamphlet or handout.

Teachers may provide family members with the following questions to ask:

- Can you tell me why this piece of work is important to you?

- Why did you chose this piece of work for your SLC? What does it say about you?

- What did you learn from that assignment? Is there anything you might have changed?

- How can we support you in your learning?

- What will help you address your academic goals?

- What are you most proud of?

- What has been your biggest challenge and what steps have you taken to overcome it?

Take-aways

- Students take ownership over the SLC and provide their own progress report, or self assessment, to family members and teachers.

- Clear guidelines and expectations for both students and family members beget the most successful SLCs.

- SLCs are deeper conversations that use student work as evidence versus simply showing work and reporting grades.

Overall, SLCs' focus on student ownership and progress helps build a better academic community. SLCs can dramatically change the attitude and behavior of all students, especially struggling ones, because they become part of the decision making. Family members, teachers, and students come together around a student-led vision for growth, which creates a better, more self-aware citizenry.

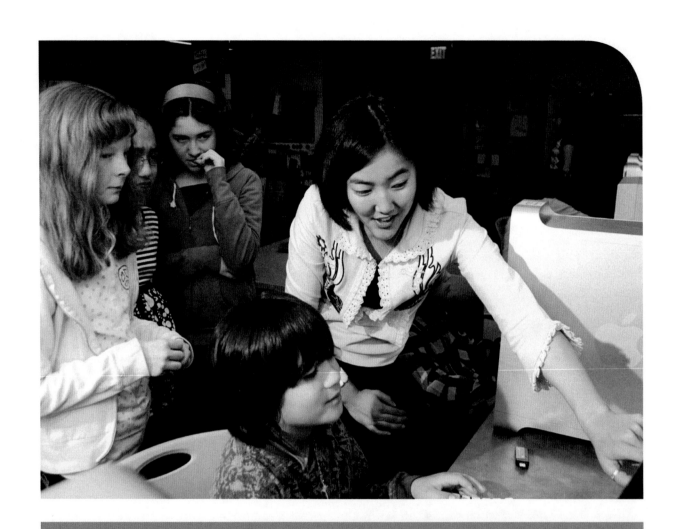

STUDENTS AND TEACHERS GENERATE MULTIPLE ITERATIONS OF THEIR WORK
INFORMED BY CRITIQUE, MODELS, OR INSTRUCTION,
IN A TRAJECTORY TOWARDS INCREASINGLY MEANINGFUL AND BEAUTIFUL WORK.

CHAPTER 3

CRITIQUE & ITERATIVE WORK

BY MICHELLE SADRENA CLARK
HIGH TECH HIGH NORTH COUNTY

CRITIQUE AND REVISION ARE *EVERYWHERE*

C ritique and revision are integral to success in the professional world. Beta versions of software depend on user review for improvement; architects' drafts are repeatedly vetted before building begins; and innovations from drugs to toys are tested for safety before being released to the public. The processes of critique and revision are used to improve work across a wide range of industries, including sports, computer science, architecture, medicine, engineering, fire fighting, theater, plumbing, custodial work, and so much more.

Despite the usefulness of these processes, critique and revision are seldom practiced in some school contexts. Why? The reason is complex, but due in part to an educational approach in which content is delivered directly by a teacher and rigor is often understood to be proportional to the number of standards covered in a semester.

However, in many parts of school, students regularly employ critique and revision practices. Musicians in the school orchestra listen carefully to their rehearsals and to professional performances; the sports teams analyze photos or video of their games and those of their opponents, and fine tune their approaches accordingly; the school's career technical education classes hold their work up to professional examples and ask, "What can we do better?"

Employing thoughtful critique and revision practices to facilitate deeper learning is an educational responsibility. When participating in the critique process, students are no longer benchwarmers or spectators to their education; they become key players in the game. Imagine a school whose student body is dedicated to personal and professional growth through the meaningful critique of real world projects in every class. Such widescale practice not only impacts student growth; it is transformative for the school as a whole. A school-wide practice of critiquing projects and subsequently revising them in an ongoing trajectory toward ever more beautiful work fundamentally impacts the school's entire culture, exponentially increases the reach and power of individual educators, brings innovation to the curriculum, and increases the likelihood of deep, lasting learning for all students.

CRITIQUE IS PERSONAL: MARIA—STUDENT AT HIGH TECH HIGH NORTH COUNTY

At the beginning of ninth grade, Maria despised critique. She felt "attacked" and felt like people were simply telling she was "not good enough." Maria found it particularly challenging to receive critique on her writing which she felt was "very honest and personal." She would read the critical feedback, take it personally, cry, and find herself and her work diminished. Maria said, "I felt that every time I was proud of something the teacher or someone else had something else I could fix or do better."

Eventually, Maria asked her teacher, "Why do I have to rearrange it if all of the information is basically there?"

The teacher responded, "Your writing is going to be shared with the community. People you know, and other that you don't know, will read it, and see your name on it. Don't you want it to be the best that it can be?"

Maria's teacher noticed that she was still hurt so she decided to share her own experience with critique, from her doctoral program. She told Maria that, rather than view critique as a personal attack, she could view it evidence of support from her peers. Maria's teacher added, "Providing someone else with critique means that people care enough about you and your work to invest time in its improvement."

Now, "I see critique as an opportunity to grow as a writer and make my work better," says Maria. "Sometimes it is still hard for me to receive critique, but I just try to remember how much these people love me and how much they want me to succeed."

WHAT IS CRITIQUE?

The words "critique" and "criticism" can carry connotations of judgment, censure, or disapproval for students and teachers alike. Critique's negative implications can lead students to feel apprehensive or even refuse to share work out of a fear of being rejected or offended. If the teacher fails to acknowledge these emotions, he or she will likely lose engagement, along with the opportunity to benefit from critique. By acknowledging that feelings are delicate, teachers can help students separate the person from the product.

Students adopt a more positive view of critique when they feel it benefits their work. HTH co-founder Rob Riordan describes critique as "a conversation about getting better at what we're doing."[1] When conversations regarding critique shift from judgment and disapproval to improvement and validation of their progress and expertise, the benefits of critique begin to emerge.

Critique can also be understood as a way to understand the pieces of a product that make it successful, and how those parts fit together to make the whole. Critique involves students giving and receiving feedback on pieces, stages, or components of a product, which gives each step or section significance. In this way, critique offers a way to positively and productively analyze products and processes for meaning, and to focus on important learning goals. [2]

Teachers can empower students to view the critique process positively by maintaining norms and employing good procedures and structures. In doing so, the teacher introduces a powerful strategy into the class culture, one that has numerous applications and lasting positive consequences.

NORMS FOR EFFECTIVE CRITIQUE[3]

- Be kind, specific, and helpful.
- Be hard on the content and soft on the person.
- Share the air—step up, step back, and help all voices be heard.

STRATEGIES FOR ACHIEVING A POSITIVE CRITIQUE ATMOSPHERE:

- Have students write their hopes and fears related to critique on post-it notes. Then, share their hopes and fears in a class discussion and acknowledge the validity of their feelings.

- Create a community agreement regarding critique etiquette based on the hopes and fears that surfaced.

- Provide examples of effective critique regularly in class, and recognize instances where they naturally occur.

- Have students critique professional work samples, or even the teacher's work, before critiquing student work.

- Debrief critique sessions and help students identify and share examples of times that they stayed true to community norms.

Critique and classroom culture work together: effective critique is fundamentally collaborative and bonds students and teachers together in a relationship in which each individual is invested in the group's success. As such, the ideal classroom environment for successful critique is both a safe space and a brave space. By nature, some students tend to avoid situations in which ideas are challenged, talent is judged, or work is scrutinized; others crave this space to validate their work. Others like to give feedback but are not comfortable receiving it; still other students are simply quiet and unsure of how to proceed. Furthermore, questions of equity arise in critical environments: Who has the power to speak and why? Who gets to define what good work looks like? Who receives the most positive feedback and why? To confront these issues, the students and teacher must create a safe place where trust is encouraged, vulnerability is considered a strength, and thoughtful contributions are celebrated for the success they bring to the group.

While achieving all of this in a single critique session might seem a juggling act, a few ideas teachers might keep in mind will help.

C.A.R.E. FOR CRITIQUE

CREATE AND MAINTAIN AN ENVIRONMENT OF TRUST

Everyone in the class is a custodian of its culture. In addition to establishing norms, teachers model appropriate critique. They must recognize when students are empathetic and supportive in critique sessions, and help the class build on these examples. To this end, mitigate hierarchical relationships through norms and protocols and look out for imbalances in the classroom's social dynamics. When teachers model the positive and constructive nature of critique and recognize when students do the same, it helps everyone learn how to contribute to future critique sessions.

ALLOW STUDENTS TO SEE THE REAL YOU

Teachers who honestly and openly share how they learn from critical feedback are models for students to engage in the same practice. By modeling how to learn from mistakes, teachers demonstrate how to receive critical feedback and what to do with it or how to apply it to the next draft. Unpacking mistakes that lead to learning, vocalizing self-doubt and wonderings, and saying those dreaded words, "I don't know!" allows teachers to give their students permission to engage in similar self-revelations.

RESPOND TO THE DIVERSITY IN THE ROOM

In a classroom of distinctly unique learners—each with his or her own set of interests, passions, past experiences in school, hopes for the future, and individual personalities—thoughtfully applied critique practices can be a path for each student to succeed. Get ready to try varied methods to encourage all voices to contribute to critique sessions. Great critique sessions depend on each student having a clear sense of their own personal goals, and knowing what to look for in other student's work.

ENCOURAGE AND EXPECT GROWTH FROM ALL STUDENTS

Some students come to class already feeling far behind their peers—why should they do one more draft if it seems like they will never catch up? Others arrive feeling able to meet the teacher's expectations in just one draft, perhaps completed on the way to school—if that earns an "A," why should they accept critical feedback? All students, regardless of perceived academic ability or past academic histories, grow when assessment systems explicitly value mastery, effort and growth and critique creates drafts in service of work destined for a valued audience.

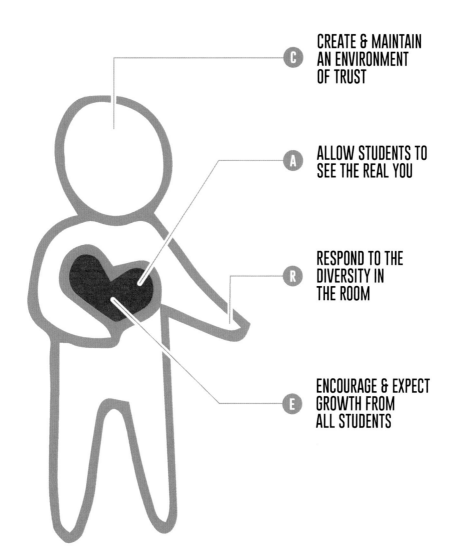

C CREATE & MAINTAIN AN ENVIRONMENT OF TRUST

A ALLOW STUDENTS TO SEE THE REAL YOU

R RESPOND TO THE DIVERSITY IN THE ROOM

E ENCOURAGE & EXPECT GROWTH FROM ALL STUDENTS

105

CRITIQUE IS POSSIBLE!

There is a great deal of power in encouraging and celebrating critique practices that move students and their work forward. Author of *An Ethic of Excellence*, EL Education Chief Academic Officer, and longtime teacher Ron Berger states, "With each iteration, confidence and self esteem are achieved through accomplishments instead of compliments."[4] However, when critique is comprised of compliments that lack substance, the process lacks sincerity and is less useful as a result. When feedback is found to be questionable, students lose faith in the process. To make critique possible, focus on establishing and maintaining norms, and use protocols to strive for equity.

BE KIND, SPECIFIC, AND HELPFUL

Berger makes a compelling case for students and teachers to be **kind, specific, and helpful** when engaging in critique. Before every critique session, share the rationale behind this language. Being kind means being empathetic to the person receiving critical feedback. Being specific requires to be precise and target exactly which parts of the work sample are done well, and which parts can be improved. Being helpful involves supporting each other in creating beautiful, meaningful work. Explain to students that critique may take many different forms and formats (verbal or written, individual or group, public or private, by novices or experts). In all of these, the purpose of critique is to develop high quality work and bond the class into a team that is invested in each other's success.

It is important that critical feedback integrates kind, specific, and helpful qualities, ideas, comments and tone. Without **kindness**, students disengage from the critique process because it hurts their self-esteem. However, critique that is only kind lacks precise information about what aspects of the work are successful and which need to improve. As such, a good critique calls for feedback that **specifically** analyzes the work's components and its learning goals. And yet simply pointing out an area of concern does not offer suggestions for how it might be improved. As such, good critique also features **helpful** suggestions for improvement, how students can build on success, and how they might inch closer to their goals. It is the intersectionality of being kind, specific, and helpful that yields the greatest results.

Once students see the value the critique process offers their work, there is a natural, grassroots commitment to the process. Teachers can facilitate student buy-in using a few simple practices and protocols:

CRITIQUE WORK FROM THE ADULT WORLD.

Teachers can start by sharing a professionally created sample, or even their own work, to help students practice during the initial rounds of critique in a class. Suppose the class will create a field guide to the natural environment around school; perhaps they will create toys that involve specific physics concepts or produce a documentary video series sharing the personal histories of veterans in the community. For each of these projects, the class's first critique sessions can be aimed at relevant professional examples. Bring in one or two high quality, relevant work samples from the professional world. Challenge students to identify specific elements that make the sample successful, meaningful, and high quality. Create and display the lists of student answers to the following questions:

- What specific elements do we see in this sample that make it successful?
- What ideas and principles do we want to take for our work?
- What will we change or do differently in our work?

When critiquing a professionally published field guide, for example, students might

SAMPLE STUDENT CRITIQUE GUIDELINES
- The goal is not to make the person bitter but to make our work better.
- Be positive. Critique is intended to help, and we build from our strengths.
- Etiquette matters. Pay attention to tone.
- Everyone has distinct and valuable perspective.
- Stay open to all possibilities for improvement.
- Stick with the norms:
  - Be kind, specific and helpful.
  - Be hard on the content and soft on the people.
  - Share the air—step up, step back, and help all voices be heard.

appreciate the photography or how the writing shares biological, geographic, and historical research. However, they may feel that specific topics need to change, that the order of the book does not work for their needs or note that they would like to see interviews with different types of experts. They may also want to change the length of a specific article or chapter, while following the basic standards that they see in professional narrative nonfiction writing. They may want to combine favorite elements from multiple professional samples to create a student version that is informed by what they took away from the professional work.

Once students have practiced critique as a form of analysis, move on to critiquing student work. Student work that can be understood by peers relatively quickly—such as visual work like blueprints, photography, some mathematical work, or even a short piece of writing—benefits from various forms of a gallery-style critique. The "Two Glows and a Grow" protocol focuses on sharing feedback about what is done well and what can improve, and skews the overall quantity of feedback toward building on strengths.

TWO GLOWS AND A GROW POST-IT CRITIQUE

1. Student work is displayed throughout the room, on the walls, or on tables.

2. Students are reminded of a specific learning goal, such as composition techniques in visual art, a particular literary device for written work, or a design constraint for engineers. A professional example or other high quality model is helpful to orient all students towards outstanding work.

3. Each student is given several post-its and a pen or pencil.

4. Students are directed to move through the space, observe work, then use their post-it to write down "Two Glows" (two pieces of warm, positive feedback that precisely label outstanding elements of other student work and articulate why they are appreciated) and a "Grow" (one kind, helpful, specific suggestion for improvement).

5. Students place the post-it on or near the analyzed work.

6. The protocol is complete when each piece of student work has "Two Glows" and one "Grow." The work is then returned to its creator and they get to read the kind, specific, and helpful feedback it received. Make it a point to facilitate an equitable distribution of feedback—it is not fair if some students receive all of the positive feedback and others receive only suggestions of what to change. Stepping in and providing feedback of your own helps model best practices.

7. Students read their feedback and ask clarifying questions to better understand which steps to next take.

8. Students revise their work based on the critique they received.

If a teacher's class is doing a group project, then a useful protocol for lowering the pressure that students sometimes feel at first critiques is to have the class work in groups to critique of one group's current draft. This type of critique allows students to discuss the merits and shortcomings of work created by a group of students in small groups before sharing with the whole class. With the critique work is done in small groups, each individual can more comfortably give feedback. An additional benefit occurs when the whole class is involved, critical feedback is softened through group presentation. And, other students can mentally prepare for when it is their group's turn to have their work critiqued—they can consider how they will share their work, and how they will respond to feedback, as they are part of their peers' process. This critique protocol is ideal for students still adjusting to critique.

CLASS CRITIQUE OF A GROUP PROJECT

1. A single group presents their work samples to the class, while the class is situated according to their groups. Depending on the nature of the content, it can be projected on a screen, displayed on a table, or distributed to all students. Establish a time limit, such as five minutes. The group that presents the work should explain where they are in their drafting process, what their goals are, and what challenges they currently face.

2. The reviewing groups spend five minutes discussing how to give feedback to the presenting group. Each group is responsible for both identifying specific elements of a draft that are clearly on the trajectory towards success, and precisely articulating steps to take to address challenges or solve problems in their work.

3. Each reviewing group then shares their variety of feedback, including "warm" comments that identify elements that are successful, and "cool" feedback, that focus on what is problematic and how to improve.

4. The whole class, including the presenting group takes two minutes to reflect on what they heard, and identify the most helpful pieces of feedback.

5. The presenting group takes approximately two minutes to respond and share their plan for revision.

6. Repeat the process for all remaining groups

TEACHERS NEED PRACTICE WITH CRITIQUE ALSO!
LORILEE NIESEN & TUNING PROTOCOLS IN CRANE SCHOOLS

Lorilee Niesen is Agriculture, Natural Resources, & Food Production Coordinator for Capital Region Academies for the Next Economy (CRANE). In her summer professional development workshop series entitled "PBL: Making it Happen," Lorilee discovered the value of project tuning protocols in eliciting effective critique that benefits the entire group. She explained that "[Tuning protocols are] unique because it's not your typical brainstorm. It allows people to be mindful and thoughtful with the words that they use."

When Lorilee introduced the project tuning protocol to a group of teachers who attended the first PBL workshops in June, they were hesitant to share their work, fearful that their project ideas were not developed enough to receive critique from colleagues. However, by the end of the protocol, Lorilee was proud to report that "they loved it!" Reflecting on their facilitation as professional development leaders, Lorilee and her team made adjustments in how they shared the tuning protocol process with the group and, during their August workshops, they were unable to accommodate the overwhelming number of teachers who wanted to have their projects tuned. In fact, in the post-workshop evaluations, teachers expressed that the tuning protocols were their "biggest takeaway." Not surprisingly, this method of facilitating critique has permeated all twenty-two schools in the consortium in various ways, including via project tuning groups, as a method for running department meetings, and as a practice to share in school trainings.

Recently, Lorilee was at a leadership meeting with school administrators from four county offices of education and eighteen school districts. They were trying to decide how to spend the remaining 1.5 million dollars of a grant they had received and Lorilee utilized a tuning protocol process to hear, analyze and reflect on specific ideas of how best to spend the funds. The leaders found the process so valuable that they left the meeting eager to implement it in their own schools. CTE Director and Principal of Washington Unified at Bryte High School used it with her staff the very same day and emailed Lorilee to share her success. Lorilee's innovative use of the tuning protocol inspired leaders to think about the diverse use of the practice.

TUNING PROTOCOLS IN CLASS

Teachers often critique their project plans, and those of their colleagues, via the tuning protocol found in Chapter One.[5] This protocol can be modified for various grade levels or ages. Tuning protocols are tools for equity—they create space for a group to focus on a student's work; they follow a linear pattern in which the group seeks to understand the work sample through explanations and questions before actually critiquing it; and they are intended to focus on the questions that the presenter—typically the student who created the work—brings to the table.

Two variations of the tuning protocol are shared on pages 114-117: a fifteen-minute version and a seven-minute version.

In the fifteen-minute version of the protocol, the teacher may arrange students into groups of four. In these groups, with effective time management, the entire class may have their work critiqued, and critique the work of three peers in just over one hour. This is intended to fit into a block class period and allows time for students to do a warm up, collect work samples to be reviewed, and create plans for, or get right to work on, their next drafts.

The seven-minute version of the protocol is intended for students in younger grades or those who are new to these types of protocols.

NORMS:

- Be kind, specific, and helpful.
- Be hard on the content and soft on the person.
- Share the air—step up, step back, and help all voices be heard.

THE PROTOCOL:

Arrange students in groups of four; the teacher acts a class-wide facilitator and timekeeper.

PROJECT OVERVIEW (3 MIN)

The presenter gives an **overview of their idea** and shares his/her thinking about key design issues. The presenter will likely share drafts, plans, or other artifacts to help the group understand his/her ideas. The presenter should share a dilemma or question he/she is working on. *Participants are silent.*

GROUP THINK TIME (1 MIN)

Participants write ideas about **what they want to know more about and ideas for the presenter.** *Presenter is silent; participants do this work silently.*

CLARIFYING QUESTIONS (2 MIN)

Participants ask **clarifying questions** of the presenter. These questions help the group more readily understand the presenter's idea. Clarifying questions tend to have brief, factual answers (i.e., "I will do three interviews," or "My rocket will have four large fins.")

PROBING QUESTIONS (2 MIN)

Participants ask **probing questions** of the presenter. Probing questions reveal the presenter's thinking and logic. They tend to start with "how" or "why."

DISCUSSION (5 MIN)

Participants begin with **positive feedback** and then identify opportunities for growth. How might the presenter need our help? What are the strongest or most exciting parts of this idea—and how might we build on these? Will we be able to complete this idea in class? Does this idea come from a real problem or need? *During this time, the presenter physically pulls him/herself back from the group, is silent, and takes notes. Participants should direct their comments to each other, not the presenter. The facilitator may need to remind participants of the presenter's dilemma question.*

REFLECTION (2 MIN)

The presenter has the **opportunity to respond** to the discussion. The presenter may share what struck him/her and what next steps might be taken as a result of the ideas generated by the discussion. *Participants are silent.*

SEVEN-MINUTE PROJECT TUNING

NORMS:

- Be kind, specific, and helpful.
- Be hard on the content and soft on the person.
- Share the air—step up, step back, and help all voices be heard.

THE PROTOCOL:

Arrange students in groups of four; the teacher acts a class-wide facilitator and timekeeper.

PROJECT OVERVIEW (1 MIN)

The presenter gives an **overview of their idea** and shares his/her thinking about key design issues. *Participants are silent.*

GROUP THINK TIME (1 MIN)

Participants write ideas about **what they want to know more about and ideas for the presenter.** *Presenter is silent; participants do this work silently.*

CLARIFYING QUESTIONS (1 MIN)

Participants ask **clarifying questions** of the presenter. These help the group understand the presenter's idea more easily. Clarifying questions tend to have brief, factual answers.

DISCUSSION (3 MIN)

Participants begin with **positive feedback** and then identify *opportunities for growth.* How might the presenter need our help? What are the strongest or most exciting parts of this idea—and how might we build on these? Will we be able to complete this idea in class? Does this idea come from a real problem or need? *During this time, the presenter physically pulls him/herself back from the group, is silent, and takes notes. Participants should direct their comments to each other, not the presenter. The facilitator may need to remind participants of the presenter's dilemma question.*

REFLECTION (1 MIN)

The presenter has the **opportunity to respond** to the discussion. The presenter may share what struck him/her and what next steps might be taken as a result of the ideas generated by the discussion. *Participants are silent.*

CRITICAL CONCERN: IS THERE ENOUGH TIME TO THOUGHTFULLY IMPLEMENT CRITIQUE IN THE CLASSROOM?

RON BERGER EXPLAINS:

"I feel like time is always the impediment. It's the biggest constraint for all of us. I think we all, as educators, can be fairly short-sighted about what's going to be memorable, what's going to really change kids, in the end. Which means that sometimes we need to carve out time to make the work the kids are doing really strong even if it means covering fewer things, and that trade-off in the end is better. At the end of that fifth grade year or eleventh grade year, that student will remember having done that math work really well, written that paper really well, understood those historical concepts really well; created something beautiful and meaningful. They will have long forgotten the many other things that you would have covered had you stayed on point. To repeat: I don't believe we should try to cover everything they we're trying to cover. I think we all try to cover too much. It's not our fault. That's the pressure on us. We need to get off that treadmill and hone some things well so that kids get a sense of how to do things well: how to do math well, how to write well, how to do research well. That means taking time for critique. When people say they don't have the time, it's because they're covering so much. We all are. We have to carve out the time; we have to take charge of our own time."[6]

AUTHENTIC WORK

Authenticity drives critique, drafting, and revision. Authenticity occurs when the product has a larger purpose, when somebody wants the information, when there is a clear audience for the product, or someone will enjoy the results of its production. When students connect their studies to the world in ways that are personally meaningful, they are more likely to be motivated to thoroughly analyze their work and the work of others, accept critical feedback, and create further drafts of ever more beautiful work. Authentic work merits critique because the final products are important to others. As Rob Riordan states, "Critique is about quality of work, but it's also about audience."[7]

Sometimes the motivation to improve a work initially stems from a student's fear of being embarrassed in front of that audience. However, embarrassment quickly gives way to progress as the student's motivation becomes based on their pride of accomplishing something of higher quality and greater usefulness.

While the mere fact of having an audience necessitates critique and revision, the usefulness of these processes are magnified when students are tasked with creating products that positively impact others' lives. Projects launched in service of elderly people, homeless individuals, children, or animals heighten the need to make good work. Similarly, products that help a local business, nonprofit organization, or those that address local social or environmental issues bring a sense of urgency and commitment to critique and revision.

With the stakes high, students need to know what makes professional work successful. They may not know what qualifies as professional standards; they may not believe they can get there; or, in some cases, their opinion of what constitutes great work may differ from the teacher's. Students should be shown examples of exemplary professional work and articulate specific learning goals by inquiring about and analyzing its components.

Mentor Examples: The Magic in Mimicry

Although the critique of professional work was described above as a method to introduce critique practices to the classroom, the concept of analyzing high quality work samples—known as "mentor examples"—is a valuable practice that should be used widely in many contexts. Mentor examples constitute any professional product, such as objects, machines, texts, art, publications, multimedia, and even performances such as songs, plays, debates, or speeches. Mentor examples help students (and teachers!) see how learning goals are integrated into successful real-world projects; mentor examples can be the inspiration for assessment devices such as checklists or rubrics; and mentor examples help students to develop the thinking and language of both academia and the professional workplace.[8]

Ron Berger explains that he uses mentor examples from professionals, teachers, community members and other students at the start of a project. "We critique and discuss what makes the work powerful: what makes a piece of creative writing compelling and exciting; what makes a scientific or historical research project significant and stirring; what makes a novel mathematical solution so breathtaking."[9]

GUIDELINES FOR CRITIQUING A MENTOR EXAMPLE

1. Teachers or students select the appropriate mentor example.

2. With guidance from the teacher, students answer specific questions designed to deconstruct the mentor example and identify what makes it high quality work. Example questions may be:

    - What makes this sample stand out as high quality?

    - What design elements work well in this genre?

    - What makes this example stand the test of time?

    - What makes this example be regarded as aesthetically pleasing?

    - Why do other professionals look to this work as a good example?

    - What specific principles or standards can we take from this for our class?

3. Students use the mentor example to discover and articulate the steps, requirements, and parameters involved in production. Teachers facilitate these discoveries and articulations through clarifying and probing questions. Ask students to show specific pieces of the work in great detail that they identify as successful. Prod them to precisely state their reasoning. Record and share kind, specific and helpful statements made by students—they are creating a shared understanding of how they will create work that is similar to that of professionals.

4. Students share their discoveries to collectively arrive at a blueprint or set of principles to follow so that their work is closely aligned to that of professionals, regardless of the students' age or previous experience.

5. Once students have deconstructed the mentor example and created their own blueprint or design principles to follow, they decide on immediate next steps to take in their own work, and long term goals for their projects. Students begin work on their next draft.

6. Once student drafts are completed, students can engage in a critique process to clarify and refine their plans for the next iteration.

PEER AND EXPERT CRITIQUE IN MUSIC PRODUCTION

James Snyder teaches AP Calculus, Integrated Mathematics II, STEM 2, and Music Production at Anderson Valley Junior and Senior High School, a small rural school located in Mendocino County, approximately two hours north of San Francisco.

In his Music Production class, students created original string quartet compositions using music notation software. During initial critique, students took turns listening to each other's music using the computer program software, then wrote kind, specific, and helpful feedback on post-its. The students took the lessons from the first round of critiques to revise their compositions.

During the second round of critique, James invited a local composer and a professional string quartet performer to play the students' original compositions in front of the class. Then the composer provided expert critique of the student compositions. The students were delighted and James also filmed the critique sessions so that his students could return to the feedback as they went about revising their composition.

"BRING IN THE EXPERTS" CRITIQUE

This high-stakes critique event occurs when an outside expert reviews, discusses, and critiques student work. In the process, students can learn professional vocabulary and gather more information regarding the context of the work, including the complexity of dealing with real-world variables and consequences. Expert feedback is typically valued by students and regarded as highly informative and technically important.

1. Identify what types of professionals or experts you need for your specific project.

2. Contact one (or more) professionals or experts in the field and invite them to your class to share expertise and critique student work.

3. Use a specific protocol, so that the expert is integrated into the class culture.

   a. Share a tuning protocol with the expert in advance, or use a gallery-style protocol.

   b. Let the expert fully share his or her ideas while maintaining classroom norms.

4. Record experts' feedback via video, audio, and/or written notes, and share it with the class or post it for all to see. Expert visitors may not have time to critique every work sample, so it is especially important that all students be able to return to their insight and instructions later in the project.

5. Invite the experts back to see the final products.

CRITICAL CONCERN: DO STUDENTS HAVE THE COMPETENCE, CONFIDENCE, OR THE SKILLS IN THE SUBJECT TO OFFER MEANINGFUL CRITIQUE?

RON BERGER EXPLAINS:

"Peer to peer critique is typically a waste of time unless kids have developed some expertise in what they're critiquing. Sometimes teachers say to kids, "Go with your writing partner and give them some critique on their piece." They're fifteen years old, they're seven years old—they're not teachers yet, they don't know how to give wise critique out of the blue if they have not studied quality for a specific dimension of the work. On the other hand, if you have just spent a day looking at strong openings and hooks, or figurative language, or strong closings, or how to write an abstract for a scientific report, and you've looked at models and you've critiqued them and you thought about what makes a good one—the dimensions of quality—kids can actually name what they value in these models from the genre. Then you can say, "Meet with your partner and look at their opening, (or their abstract, their closing, their use of figurative language...)" Kids have just been steeped in expertise in that, they know the language of it, they know the dimensions of what they value in it. They can offer kind, specific and helpful critique."[10]

COLLABORATIVE DESIGN THROUGH CRITIQUE

Teachers and students can begin to collaboratively design rubrics with their very first critique. The moment a class critiques a professional piece of work and engages in the process of articulating what makes it high quality, they start to co-create a list of qualities they hope to achieve in their own work.

This list can help determine whether student work meets collaboratively determined requirements that were the result of critique. It can guide ongoing development of various drafts, as students press further into their projects. Once students are well into the process, these qualities and characteristics can be expanded, annotated with definitions of quality, to become a collaboratively designed rubric.

To collaboratively design a rubric, teachers must relinquish some control over what counts, and for how much. When teachers engage students as co-constructors of rubrics through critique protocols, they democratize the learning experience.

That said, certain standards of excellence remain non-negotiable, and teachers must guide students to see these standards when they critique mentor examples. When critiquing a professional sample, help students see what may become rubric categories, and help show how professionals understand their relative significance to each other. Likewise, it is critical that students and teachers justify their suggestions throughout the process by pointing to evidence in mentor examples during critique protocols.

CO-CONSTRUCT A RUBRIC THROUGH CRITIQUE

Developing a shared rubric via critique processes can take time—teachers and students need to discover and articulate the categories, the descriptors, and the relative values—and for teachers who teach multiple classes per day, this task can be daunting. There are a few ways to resolve this:

- At first, strive to collaboratively create a checklist, not a complete rubric, via critique.

- Take your time. This does not need to be completed in one class period.

- Use a dedicated team of students—perhaps the whole class should be involved in creating the initial checklist, and then a few students come together for the rest, and the rest of the class approves or comments on a draft of the rubric.

- Do what works! Creating the absolutely perfect, fail-safe rubric is difficult—focus on using critique to include diverse student voices in articulating what great work looks like. Don't let a desire for the perfect rubric be the enemy of embracing critique to include students in collaboratively designing assessment tools.

GUIDELINES TO CONSTRUCT A RUBRIC THROUGH CRITIQUE

1. The teacher and students critique mentor examples and create a list of elements found in established, professional work.

2. The class narrows this list to a set of requirements for achieving high-quality work.

3. The teacher and students cluster ideas into logical and cohesive rubric categories.

4. The teacher and students discuss what different levels of achievement would look like for each category, developing descriptors and examples. Students may create written examples first.

5. The teacher and students discuss the relative significance of each category to determine each category's weight. Students may want to write their reasons and supporting arguments.

6. Students use the rubric—or a draft of it—to assess peers' latest revision of work.

CRITICAL CONCERN: DO STUDENTS LIKE CRITIQUE?

RON BERGER EXPLAINS:

"The first thing I would say is I think it's a big mistake to think of critique only as formal peer-to-peer critique. Peer-to-peer critique is an important part of the critique culture of your classroom. Once your classroom is functioning well in a culture of critique, however, most of the useful peer to peer critique is informal when you don't even know it's going on. The formal peer-to-peer critique protocols are hard to fit in regularly so they're not going to happen all the time. The informal peer-to-peer critique should be ubiquitous in your classroom because you've built that culture where they want it all the time and want to give it all the time. Both of those, to go well, are dependent on you as the teacher modeling useful critique in Critique Lessons. So, if peer critique is not going well in your classroom, the first thing I would ask is how much you have modeled it in Critique Lessons that you are leading. I always distinguish between peer-to-peer critique (or teacher-to-student critique) in service of moving a particular piece of work or understanding forward, from a whole class or small group Critique Lesson. A Critique Lesson is not in service of improving a particular piece of work, but instead to examine models of work—from students or professionals—to build understanding of what quality looks like in that genre. We are not looking for flaws for but for strengths to borrow and use ourselves. Those are two separate things to me. Both are important."[11]

CRITIQUE TOWARDS EQUITY

Equity is defined and interpreted in many different ways, but in its broadest sense, equity means that everyone feels valued regardless of race, gender, sexuality, or physical or cognitive ability. In any given classroom, there are a plethora of cognitive and academic strengths that need to be developed. Too often, struggling students are patronized instead of receiving constructive critique that can improve their learning experience. Though well intentioned, these affirming responses do very little to develop a student's skills.

Thus, the first step in practicing equitable critique is for teachers to establish a fully participatory culture in which every single student gives and receives feedback. While student differences should be kept in mind, labels such as "struggling" or "talented" are inaccurate and unhelpful to academic and social development. Consider a student's ability as fluid depending on the subject, their skill set, and their emotional outlook. A student who struggles to write an organized essay may excel in public speaking; likewise, a student who feels challenged by mathematical word problems may find success in conducting experiments and analyzing spreadsheet data. Just as every student has room for growth, every student also exhibits a skill in something. Through effective teacher modelling and practicing critique, students will learn to recognize the wide variety of gifts and growth areas in the room.

Critique and iterative work are a means of achieving equity. The critique process gives students voice in proceedings, and in doing so offers students self-efficacy. When students feel their voice is important, the teacher has taken a valuable step towards creating a more equitable classroom. In classrooms that value equity, students are empowered to contribute their varying perspectives. Not only does this broaden the class's understanding of what is worthy of assessment, it challenges the classroom's traditional power dynamic. The teacher is no longer the sole judge and jury; rather, both student and teacher input have value. Such empowered critique sessions leave everyone with more ideas, new questions, broader possibilities, and better odds for arriving at an authentic product.

Progressive educators deliberately design projects that bring together diverse learners. Grouping students in heterogeneous critique groups is imperative to achieving the equity-driven classroom. This means that critique groups should reflect mixed genders, races, socioeconomic status, ability, and perspectives. The rich experiences, backgrounds, and social and academic skills that characterize heterogeneous groups provide more thoughtful, provocative, and scintillating critique.

Moreover, diverse critique groups mirror real-life work in that professional colleagues are often from a variety of backgrounds and possess a variety of skills. When project-based learning groups are comprised of a variety of students with different interests and abilities, their work ends up adopting the processes and qualities that professional teams and work groups have found paramount to success.

CRITIQUE PEER ROUNDS (CPR)

This protocol is designed to create space for every student to answer questions from their perspective about their peers' work.

1. Have each student select one specific piece of work to share for critique. Set up the room so that each student can focus on one specific piece of work.

2. Select the format to give and receive critical feedback: via conversation, sticky notes, on a single sheet of paper, etc.

3. Typically, CPR rounds are approached with an asset-minded perspective, so that students identify specific strengths in one another's work, and recommend ways to build on strengths. Share this norm with the group.

4. Pose one specific question to the class. You may say the question to the class and/or post the question in writing. Example questions include:

    *   How does the photograph relate to the author's text?

    *   How does the toy design appear to meet the needs of the child who will receive it?

    *   What is the most compelling piece of scientific data in this documentary?

5. Instruct the class to share two levels of feedback:

    *   Identify at least one specific positive elements of the work, and:

    *   Kindly explain one specific way for the work to be improved.

6. Rotate the students to new work samples. At this point, you can pose a new question or ask the next students to return to the original question. Regardless, direct the students to avoid providing the same feedback as the previous student. If a student claims that the only feedback that he or she wishes to offer is support of the previous student's comment, then focus his or her efforts on articulating specific, personal reasons why.

7. Repeat the CPR process several times, rotating students every time. Each time students rotate, remind them that it is each individual's perspective that is valuable.

TOTAL TIME: APPROXIMATELY 2-3 MINUTES PER ROUND

RON BERGER EXPLAINS:

"The first thing I would say is I think it's a big mistake to think of critique only as peer-to-peer critique. So peer-to-peer critique is an important part of the critique culture of your classroom. To be honest though, once your classroom is functioning well in a culture of critique, most of the useful peer to peer critique is informal when you don't even know it's going on. The formal peer-to-peer critiques are hard to schedule time wise and, they're not going to happen all the time. The informal peer-to-peer critique should be ubiquitous in your classroom because you've built that culture where they want it all the time and want to give it all the time. Both of those, to go well, are dependent on you having modeled critique in critique lessons. So, if it's not going well, the first thing I would say is how much have you modeled it in critique lessons that you are leading? So, I would differentiate between peer-to-peer critique in service of moving a particular piece of work or understanding forward, than a whole class or small group critique lesson in which the critique is used to build understanding of what quality looks like in that genre. Those are two separate things to me. They overlap but they're separate." [11]

STRIVING FOR THE FINAL DRAFT

Equitable, productive critique and revision experiences don't coalesce overnight; they take commitment to classroom norms; good use of protocols; and the understanding of professional samples and diverse perspectives. Teachers have to be willing to leave behind expectations that they are the sole arbiter of quality or the lone voice of instruction. But once they do, there is a world to be gained as students embrace their full identity as learners.

Teachers may find that incorporating critique and revision into their classrooms happens organically over time, as they embrace other elements of project-based learning. After all, critique and revision are typically found throughout the school already—imagine the student musician listening carefully to a mentor, striving to correct seemingly minute details in his performance; imagine the student athlete working with a coach to carefully adjusting her footwork to match that of an admired professional star; imagine the student journalist pitching a draft of a story to class, listening for feedback so that the story will be ready for prime time in the school news. These are examples of critique that can be brought into any classroom. Doing so does not require a complete overhaul of practices; most teachers find they can start small. They might choose just one project component to critique and revise, and they will open up opportunities for deeper learning for all students. Once confidence in the process is established, it will feel comfortable and productive to expand to other project elements.

Critique and iteration are already present in many areas of student and professional life, so it makes sense to capitalize on students' natural inclination to give and receive feedback. Not only will teachers increase engagement, opportunity, achievement, and facilitate the production of high-quality work, they will cultivate a generation of students ready for the level of revision and refinement required in the real world.

Ryan Mammarella, an English teacher at Morro Bay High School, realized that "changing perception is hard, but it starts with understanding what the current perception is." He started by having an open dialogue with his students about critique and what they thought of when they heard the words like "peer review."

"They were very honest with me." Ryan said, "They openly admitted that they felt peer review was 'pointless,' was a result of teachers being 'lazy,' and that peer review days usually ended up just being days where they talked about the football game over the weekend or a party at a friends house."

Ryan realized that he needed to go back to square one and he started doing simple protocols. He started with protocols designed to generate focused, concrete feedback to ensure productive critique sessions. He then pushed his students and the protocols towards more abstract, bigger-picture questions of content and style. Ryan was careful to keep the critique sessions focused on the work, not the individual students.

Ryan explained, "One of the biggest changes I emphasized when working with students on providing feedback was to talk about the work as if the person or people who created it was not present. In other words, make the work central in order to provide honest and consistent feedback." Ryan suspected that the challenge stemmed from the perception that a new type of work was now expected in the classroom, and students were unsure if critique sessions would generate results for them. However, he notes that "Once the perception started to change, review protocols became more complex and ultimately more successful."

INTERNSHIPS, EXTERNSHIPS, AND SERVICE LEARNING OFFER STUDENTS THE OPPORTUNITY TO EXPAND AND ENLARGE THEIR IDENTITIES.

CHAPTER 4

COMMUNITY PARTNERSHIPS

BY COLLEEN GREEN, PH.D.
HIGH TECH HIGH INTERNATIONAL

WHEN *STUDENTS* AND *COMMUNITY* MEET

Bright sunlight shines across San Diego bay and through oversized studio windows, right onto Matthew's office desk. Matthew is a junior at High Tech High International, but for almost one month, he is interning with a local communications and design firm, and he has just returned from an office team meeting. With a coffee mug in one hand and pad of paper in the other, Matthew looks he could be any one of the firm's employees, all of whom are college graduates.

Matthew developed a love of graphic design during a sophomore year project, when a staff member of this communications firm formed a community partnership with the class and mentored students through their design process. That experience led Matthew to pursue graphic design for his internship—a graduation requirement for all HTH students—even though it was not directly related to marine science, his anticipated college major. During internship, Matthew worked alongside mentors who were trained in graphic design, creating actual content for clients in San Diego and Los Angeles.

While graphic design was not Matthew's intended career path, the internship opened new opportunities and taught him a great deal about himself as both a student and an individual. He learned how he functions as a team member and realized how important it is to love one's work. "That is something I want to bring with me throughout life," Matthew reflects. "I don't want to ever wake up and say, 'ugh, work'. I want to find something that I'll enjoy doing throughout however long I'll have to work."

Internship also provided Matthew insight into his own work habits, which will help him as he transitions to college. "Sometimes I'd be working on one task or multiple tasks and I really had to manage my time because due dates are due dates," he says. "Not making the due date is very unprofessional and then it hurts the company's reputation, which then ruins how people see me." Matthew also learned how the post-high school world functions. "I learned how to connect with clients," he says, "You have to be on the same page with them and really know what they want in order to create something creative and very professional. I had no idea that was part of the graphic design industry."

Matthew's experience illustrates the benefits of community partnerships like an academic internship. Such experiences are not simply about careers, but also about the pursuit of passion in the adult world of work. Moreover, for many students—particularly those from low-income families—the internship experience represents a powerful entry into adult networks and community partnerships.

LEARNING THROUGH CONNECTION AND REFLECTION: THE VALUE OF COMMUNITY PARTNERSHIPS

Community partnerships are born when a school or classroom connects with a local organization to provide meaningful, engaging, and relevant experiences for students that also serve the needs of the organization. Community partnerships are not simply or necessarily about jobs and careers—rather, they are characterized by relationships and learning opportunities: students engage with community members to do real, meaningful work.

In a community partnership, the community becomes an extension of the classroom. The *New Urban High School: A Practitioner's Guide* explains community partnerships as experiences that "change the context for teaching and learning...situat[ing] students in the adult world of work and learning, confronting them with unpredictable situations, new perspectives that cut across subject matters, and invaluable lessons in dealing with people in the world."

While community partnerships can take several forms, this chapter will focus on three: service learning, internships, and externships.

 SERVICE LEARNING:
This teaching and learning strategy links meaningful community service to the curriculum (e.g., Biology, Engineering, Writing) while ensuring students' civic engagement focuses on strengthening the community.[1] Its duration may vary (one day, one week, one month), and it can be immersive or episodic.

 INTERNSHIP:
Internships offer a formalized, facilitated learning program that provides practical but exploratory experiences to students under the guidance of an expert in the field. Internships are based on student interests, though specific career alignment is not a requirement.

 EXTERNSHIP:
Externships are opportunities for students to explore career interests, gain professional experience, build relationships with community members, and cultivate their knowledge and skills in new areas. Students often engage in externships when they are seniors, and use the experience to connect with an adult member of the community. Externships can be less formal, more flexible experiences, and range from job shadowing to community service.

WHY CREATE COMMUNITY PARTNERSHIPS?

Community partnerships offer both school and community stakeholders something valuable. Students gain real-life experience and develop opportunities for personal reflection that emphasize the relevance of academic learning while ensuring civic engagement that is focused on strengthening the community. Moreover, "research indicates that workplace learning enhances student achievement, preparation for college, attendance, and attitude, finding that students who participate in [community partnerships] are more likely to get better grades, stay in school, go directly to college, and approach life and work with a positive attitude."[2] Meanwhile, community partners gain an opportunity to introduce their work to students, increase student excitement about that work, observe student engagement and growth in the work, and mentor students who will potentially work in these professions upon their high school or college graduation.

The goal of any school-to-community program is for benefits to be reciprocal. Students gain experience, insight, confidence, and opportunities to reflect on their learning and work; the community partner, meanwhile, gains a valuable contributing member of their organization. One National Employer Leadership Council study shows that employer benefits include "reduced recruitment costs, reduced training and supervision, reduced turnover, increased retention rates, higher productivity of students and high productivity and promotion rates of school-to-work program graduates who eventually are hired compared with those of other newly hired workers."[3] Matthew's junior internship experience offers an example of how this symbiotic relationship plays out. The student learned to transfer his skills from the classroom to the workplace, while the graphic design firm discovered an asset in someone who could produce real work for their clients.

SERVICE LEARNING AS ENGAGED LEARNING

Service learning programs start best when they start small. As Emily Pilloton, Executive Director of Project H Design and author of *Design Revolution*, puts it, "Kids are engaged any time they can identify with the thing on a personal level." While projects can involve the whole school, those undertaken by individual classes or even distinct grades of students make for stronger experiences. Smaller groups help students focus on establishing an intimate relationship with the community partner and developing it over the period of work.

Service learning projects require schools to have specific individuals with whom community partners can interface; community partners need at least one key point of contact. These contacts are critical for scheduling visits, establishing the flow of work, and fielding questions or concerns that arise before, during, or after the experience. This also helps spread capacity for future programs—a single point of contact who is intimately familiar with the school community can bridge and build future relationships.

THE BIG PICTURE: LAUNCHING SERVICE LEARNING

Teachers and schools interested in integrating a service learning component into their curriculum need to first identify which community needs can be met through student project work, and how. Students are a part of this initial conversation; this gets them immediately engaged and fosters their ownership over a community connection. Students can engage from the outset by brainstorming possible community partners, target populations, or high-profile needs.

Once needs are identified, students help articulate and design the plan to serve the community, and are fully involved in executing it. This is not a hollow activity that will be shelved once assessed or graded. According to Rob Riordan,"Internships and other forms of community work emphasize the opportunities to make authentic contributions to the community." These contributions include creating needed products or services for community partners. One example comes from High Tech High teacher David Berggren's class, where students worked with United Cerebral Palsy of San Diego to design assistive technology for patients. Jay Vavra and Tom Fehrenbacher, also of High Tech High, had students engage in long-term investigations, reflections, and publications about the San Diego Bay. They created field guides in which students served as researchers and contributed to the understanding of local ecosystems, and celebrated the work of local heroes. Students in other classrooms have served local health agencies as translators or designed websites for local elementary schools. "All of this," notes Riordan, "represents work of lasting value."

As students plan for these kinds of projects, teachers help them facilitate critique and feedback sessions with community partners to make sure they are meeting real needs. Students can use this feedback to make necessary adjustments to their work—striving for better messaging in an advertising campaign to support a local non-profit, for example, or changing the design of a remodeling project at a local community center. Through such communication and revision, students take further ownership over the project and see relationships through from start to finish.

After the project is complete and shared with the community partner, it is important to give students an opportunity to reflect on their experiences. For more on reflective practices, see Chapter 6 on reflection.

STORIES OF SERVICE: THE HTHCV TINY HOMES PROJECT

Classrooms reimagined: that's the idea at the heart of service learning projects, including one that took place in Chula Vista, California. For one year, ninth graders at High Tech High Chula Vista became architects. They partnered with Space4Art, a local organization that seeks to create thriving centers where artists can live, work, and interact with each other and their community. The students' goal was to design and ultimately build three "tiny homes" for local artists.

Classroom desks became drafting tables. Students' learning space became a vacant lot where they spent their day interfacing with the community, their clients, and each other. Students poured over art created by their clients, read and studied where each came from, and considered what inspired them. Students put this knowledge to use creating homes that reflected their clients' needs and lifestyles. Instead of tests and quizzes, assessments took the form of blueprints and client feedback.

The Tiny Homes Project encompassed three aspects of strong community partnerships. First, students recognized a need in their community. Teachers engaged their students in conversations about what was essential to the targeted community and how students could make a real impact. As one ninth grader said, "This project is bigger than us. It's about making affordable, quality housing to keep artists in our city."

Second, the project required students to deeply connect with members of the community. As a result, students realized that this was more than a school project; they were creating real living spaces for real people. To achieve a

deep understanding of their clients and appreciation of their needs, students conducted in-depth interviews with the artists. These yielded specific stories that helped students design blueprints for unique living spaces that met each artist's individual needs.

Finally, students took ownership over the project and developed skills that extend beyond the school environment. The project began at HTHCV and was originally slated to last one school year, but has since been expanded—for both the original students and the school. Students involved in the first phase of design and building have continued to work to secure funding for future building opportunities and to grow their community partnerships. Some have made this community the focal point of future projects; others chose it as the subject for their 11th grade internships and 12th grade externships. The community partnership blossomed to include work for other HTHCV students on other opportunities, like a community park.

STEPS FOR UNDERTAKING A SERVICE LEARNING INITIATIVE

1. Brainstorm and ideate with stakeholders, including students.

2. Survey the community to identify needs.

   ○ Teachers can start this work. For example, over the summer a teacher might identify that the YMCA, an environmental organization, a local homeless shelter, or a Veteran's group is willing to work with students. The teacher builds the relationship; then students connect in Step 3.

3. Connect with community partners or recipients of student work.

4. Work with community partner mentors to draft a plan for service.

   ○ Teachers facilitate this draft work, invite community partners to the classroom to serve as panelists and give feedback on the draft, and help students create a revision plan that meets the end needs of the community partner.

5. Gather feedback from community members, peers, and mentors.

6. Work with adult mentors to revise the plan.

7. Begin work.

8. Draft and revise with critical feedback from community partners, other students, and teachers.

9. Present work to community and outside adults.

10. Reflect on the work.

BREAKING IT DOWN: LOGISTICS OF THE SERVICE LEARNING PROGRAM

Service learning opportunities are most successful when they are driven by communities' needs and students' interests and are fundamentally connected to the curriculum. In addition, the most powerful service learning opportunities provide multiple and meaningful opportunities for reflection and connection—throughout the project, not just at its conclusion. All of this is achieved through intentional planning and the collaboration of classroom teachers, community partners, school administration, and even parents.

Both reflection and evaluation are important components for any service learning experience. Evaluation allows participants to provide concrete feedback on what could improve the practice. Reflection allows participants to review what they learned, explore how they changed, and examine their feelings about the experience. Students, teachers, and community partners participate in reflection exercises; they also evaluate project outcomes and processes.

KEY ISSUES TO CONSIDER WHEN PLANNING FOR A SERVICE LEARNING EXPERIENCE:

1. How will the project be funded? How long will funding last?

2. How long will the project take to plan, implement, and complete?

3. What expectations are there for students doing service? What expectations for hosting partners? What work will need to be done outside of the classroom? What materials are needed, and who is responsible for getting them?

4. What learning experiences will the teacher and/or school provide for the students before, during, and after the experience?

5. How will the service learning project be evaluated, and by whom?

1. In what ways did you grow as a result of your experience?

2. What benefits did your community partner incur as a result of your project?

3. What did you learn from the experience? How does it relate to what you are studying in school?

4. What were this project's strengths? What were its weaknesses?

5. What are some personal challenges or problems you faced during this project?

6. What advice would you give to other students for how to improve, continue, or expand the project?

INTEREST EXPLORATION: ACADEMIC INTERNSHIPS

"Internship is an experience in which a student becomes more than he or she was before."
—Rob Riordan, Co-founder of High Tech High

All High Tech High students complete an immersive academic internship. Although that experience occurs in the eleventh grade, preparation for it and reflection on it are ongoing throughout all four years of a student's high school experience. Some schools make internship opportunities available in twelfth grade, but the internship experience is more strategically placed in eleventh grade; this maximizes the potential for its post-high school impact. After all, eleventh grade is when students make critical decisions about their next steps in life—when or if to apply to college, whether to take tests like the SAT, and what life beyond school might consist of.

Above all, internship is not about tracking; nor is it about career placement. Rather, it is an eye-opening, informative experience that prepares an individual to make critical choices for the next phase of life—whatever that may be. "The purpose of an internship is not career preparation," says Rob Riordan, co-founder of High Tech High and President Emeritus of the High Tech High Graduate School of Education. "It is preparation for life after school. Internship is an experience in which a student becomes more than he or she was before." Riordan and others at HTH view internships as no less than "an expansion of identity." While internships take place in businesses and offices, and feature skills that pertain to all types of work environments, their goal is not solely to introduce students to a career. As Riordan puts it, "An internship's real purpose is to enter the world beyond school, understand how it works, and become bigger as a result of that."[4]

Internships can take many different forms, but all extend from the concept of service learning. In addition, all feature the student at the center of the work. Work takes place alongside a mentor and sees the student and mentor working collaboratively to benefit the partner organization.

Academic internships feature a fluid process. Some details must take place in a linear progression; others will be ongoing. Learning begins even before a student sets foot on the internship site. For example, identifying potential internship institutions requires a student to practice public speaking, research, and collaborative learning. Securing their internship placement requires them to learn soft skills like confidence, communication, and etiquette, and more practical skills like resume and cover letter preparation, writing and revision, and strategies for articulating goals and skills, interviewing, and time management.

In *Knowing and Doing: Connecting Learning and Work*, Lili Allen, Christopher Hogan, and Adria Steinberg situate internships around six key components and expectations:

1. Experiences are structured around learning goals agreed to by students, teachers, and partners, and that assist students in reaching school and district standards.
2. Students carry out projects that are grounded in real-world problems, take effort and persistence over time, and result in the creation of something that matters to them and has an external audience.
3. Students receive ongoing coaching and expert advice on projects and other work tasks from employers and community partners. By learning to use strategies and tools that mirror those used by experts in the field, students develop a sense of what is involved in accomplished adult performance and they begin to internalize a set of real-world standards.
4. Students develop a greater awareness of career opportunities in the field and deepen their understanding of the educational requirements of those careers.
5. Students develop their ability to use disciplinary methods of inquiry (just as scientists do) and enhance their capacity to tackle complex questions and carry out independent investigations.
6. Students are able to demonstrate their achievements through multiple assessments, including self-assessment, specific performance assessments (e.g., an oral proficiency exam), and exhibitions.[5]

When an internship program commits to these six principles, students accomplish relevant and engaging work. They also have opportunities to reflect on their own learning and the importance of their work in the community.

A student's internship experience benefits from the involvement of as many of his or her teachers as possible. School administration also plays a role, in terms of identifying the time of year during which internships will take place and the program's parameters (how many days per week internships are done, for how many hours, etc.). There are two general variations on internships: episodic semester-long experiences, in which students go to community partners up to three days per week for full or half days; and short-term immersions, in which students visit community partners for full days every day for two to four weeks.

Regardless of structure, the internship program begins with a series of strategically-timed events and supports designed to help students find, prepare for, and enter into an internship placement.

A TIMELINE FOR INTERNSHIP READINESS

To create an integrated, academic internship, students engage in the following work primarily with their core classroom teachers. That said, this work does not have to fall solely on a teacher of any specific discipline. As a school identifies its internship program's goals, all academic teachers can find a space in which to work with cohorts of students preparing for internship. Every teacher is capable of supporting the work of preparing for, and seeing through, students' experiences with academic internships.

MONTH ONE

- Students draft and revise resumes and cover letters.

- Students draft one to three cover letters tailored to various potential placements.

- Students call and/or email local internship sites to inquire about potential placements.

  - Focus on use of professional language in phone conversations and emails.

- Students learn research skills to help them find and coordinate internship placements.

- Parents are invited to an internship open house where they are introduced to the internship process.

  - Focus on the purpose of internship, basic logistics (how students will find an internship, when to expect permission slips, who can be a mentor, and other issues like student transportation, liability, and types of internships).

  - This is an ideal time for teachers to ask parents about their own workplace and if they are interested in mentoring an intern (not their own child).

MONTH TWO

- Students participate in mock job interviews.

  - Focus on interviewing skills, including body language, eye contact, professional gestures like handshakes, and how to answer questions to highlight students' skillsets.

- Students participate in real interviews for internships.

  - Build in time for students to send thank you notes and/or emails.

- Students follow up on all interviews and conversations.

- Students take home permission slips for a site visit (month three) and to embark on the overall internship experience.

MONTH THREE

- Students solidify internships and mentor relationships.
  - ○ Focus on clarifying site expectations, such how many hours students will be present per day, how many days per week, how they will track this time (i.e., via timesheets), and what happens when the student is ill or the mentor is absent.
- Students explore and plan their transportation to and from their potential internship, practicing their routes on a one-day site visit.
- Students participate in an internship site visit.
  - ○ Students begin work with mentor to identify a potential internship project or job description that will focus the intern's work (note: some mentors prefer to do this work once the internship has begun).
- Internship Mentors attend a welcome meeting run by students and teachers (and former interns and mentors).
  - ○ Focus on reiterating school supervisor roles and mentor expectations, including how often school site staff will visit, how students can reach school site staff in an emergency, and what responsibilities the intern and mentor have about site communications (e.g., what sort of daily "logging" will occur).

ONGOING

- Students investigate their interests and skills to see how these can support their internship work.

- Students are reminded of internship completion protocols such as hours per day, hours per week, and conducting presentations of learning (POLs).

  - Presentations of learning involve students creating a culminating presentation that can take place at the internship site or the school. They include the internship mentor, other colleagues from the internship placement, potentially parents, and where possible, younger students who will participate in internships the following year. Read more on POLs in Chapters 5 and 6.

  - Focus on daily expectations for interns (attendance, professional dress, respect, project attitude).

  - Focus on daily expectations for mentors (appropriate work, mentorship, availability, safe working environment for mentor and student).

There is no "best" approach to resolving every logistical challenge in having students outside of the school building and at a worksite. What works in one school or district may not work in another, due to a host of factors such as changing regulations, policies and procedures, or the fluctuating roles or personnel at community organizations. If there is a "best" approach, it is surely one that features flexibility and diversity.

CULTIVATING AND MAINTAINING COMMUNITY PARTNERSHIPS

Internship programs benefit from a few basic practices and protocols, many of which pertain to identifying and cultivating community partners. Keep the following in mind as the school's internship program is developed:

Be on the lookout for community partners. Teachers and students request contacts for community partners at back-to-school night, open house, and school conference events. While students should not intern with their parent or guardian, personal networks can provide valuable access to potential community partnerships; parents and guardians can mentor interns who do not live in their own household.

MENTORING STUDENTS AS A LONG-TERM RETURN ON INVESTMENT

"OUR ENGINEERING MENTORS SAY, 'WOW, THESE KIDS CAN DO SOMETHING AND WE CAN BE INVOLVED IN HELPING THEM IMPROVE THEIR SKILLS."
—*Brandee Brewer, Capital Region Academies for the Next Economy (CRANE)*

Students in Sacramento county are engaged in regular conversations about clean air and other environmental concerns via in-class mentorships, out-of-class pathway experiences, and internships. For example, one program brings students to a college campus where they work alongside college students, professors, and industry professionals to participate in hands-on diesel and clean air initiatives and experiments. According to Brandee Brewer, CRANE Career Specialist, many of these students walk away with a new understanding of and appreciation for higher education, sharing, "You know maybe I do want to go to college," or "Maybe this is the place for me." "Keep in mind [that] these are students who started this program not knowing what they want to do, not belonging in any way, not having found their niche," says Brewer. "Through this process ... we get them enrolled in community college classes right there."

Equally exciting for the students and the CRANE career specialists is that students work on engineering projects with professional engineers and mentors who continue to engage with students throughout the year. Mentors know that participating in such relationships does not necessarily mean a student will come work for them immediately after graduating from high school; rather, they are building relationships for long-term returns on their investment. By participating in these events, mentors "see just what the students are capable of and how they can best mentor them" in the hopes that through and even after college students may return to work with them as colleagues.

Use the school's networks to find partners. Educators across the school community can cull from their own professional networks, specifically considering adults who likely have the professional values and contextual understanding to be strong mentors or create positive internship experiences.

Maintain a living database of key contacts and internship site possibilities. Once contacts are identified, keep them in a central database that can be edited by teachers but accessed and viewed by students. Add to it often and populate it with useful information, such as multiple ways to contact a person, their associated institution, their role, and how they came to the school's attention as a potential community partner. Once this database of contacts has been established, it should be updated after every internship experience and at the beginning of each school year.

Give students a script to follow when reaching out. As students begin to contact community partners, situate them as if in a call center. Such a script might address the following questions:

- What do students say as an introduction? *Hello, my name is ____ and I'm a student at _____ school. We send students out on academic internships with our community partners and I'm calling today to see if you or anyone in your organization would be interested in hosting an intern from our school this year.*

- What if the person they reach is not who they should speak to? *Oh, ok. Do you happen to know who I could speak to about this? Would you happen to have their contact information handy?*

- What if the person on the phone wants to know more about internships? *Sure, I can tell you a bit more about our program...*

- What happens if the person says no? *Oh, ok, I understand. Thank you so much for your time. Have a wonderful day.*

HANDS & MINDS

SAFETY, SECURITY, AND SCHOOL-SPECIFIC CONSIDERATIONS

Setting up a strong internship program requires more than just finding locations and partners. Schools must also take seriously student safety, insurance, parent permission, and student transportation.

For most of these issues, working closely with school administration and the school business office can yield the necessary documentation, but each school's needs and expectations will be unique. Schools can treat the internship like a recurring field trip and use the appropriate permission forms. Or, a local school or district may offer a process to resolve logistical concerns and internship placements—if that is available, a school may choose to use that process.

REFLECTION: INTERNSHIP BLOGS, VLOGS, AND PRESENTATIONS OF LEARNING

Reflection is an essential part of the internship experience. Regular opportunities for reflection—via blogs, photo essays and vlogs (video blogs)—help students capture their daily learning experiences and provide content for longer reflections that feed into a culminating presentation of learning (POL). Daily blog prompts might consist of written responses, videos, and/or photos (or ideally, all three). These prompts can be crafted by teachers or students before internship even begins, and then rolled out daily or weekly for student response.

After internship, students present about the experience to their mentors, teachers, peers, and even families. This POL serves as a reflective capstone of the entire internship experience, and includes the work students did leading up to the internship. High Tech High students deliver these presentations at the internship site, in front of student peers, the school advisor, the site place mentor and colleagues, and often family. Students discuss their work, how they grew as a student, how they changed as a person, what skills they gained, how they will implement these, and more.

CAREER EXPLORATION:
BUILDING EXTERNSHIPS TO SUPPORT COLLEGE AND CAREER READINESS

"Externships allow students to dive deeply into the world beyond school."
—*Larry Rosenstock, Co-founder and CEO, High Tech High*

WHAT IS AN EXTERNSHIP?

Externship is a culminating academic event that takes place during a student's senior year. These in-depth, real-world experiences offer students opportunities to build on the skills they have acquired during school and internships. Some students choose to do an externship at the same firm at which they interned; others choose a different but related site or industry; still others decide to switch tracks and try something new altogether.

No matter how they craft the experience, externships provide students with a plethora of opportunities and the chance to:

Invest in relevant skills. For students who know what they want to study in college, externships provide an opportunity to hone a specific set of skills they are confident they will draw on in the near future.

Dive deep into an industry. Students who extern at a site where they interned can gain even more experience and dive deeper into a particular field. Externships also allow students to explore multiple faces of one industry. For example, a student who interned with an electrical engineer during a previous experience might use their externship to explore a different field of engineering.

Engage in advanced study. Students may engage in independent study or take college courses through externships, thus gaining a leg up on college applications and resumes.

Pursue interests and passions. Externships give students an opportunity to pursue something they are interested in but may not intend to study in college.

Experiment. Externships present an excellent opportunity for students to get a taste of an industry they are considering; they may find they want to go deeper. Or, just as useful, they may find they can entirely rule it out as a potential career path.

Grow a network. Through externships, students make invaluable connections with professional mentors who not only help them shape their project and overall learning, but also offer advice and assistance in making connections in the world beyond school.

Get real world work experience. Externships provide students opportunities to get a hands-on understanding of their declared college major before formally embarking on their course of study.

Ultimately, the goal of an externship is to give students real experience before they commit to a college major or career field. This is exceptionally critical because many colleges have moved or are moving away from allowing students to enter with "undecided" or "undeclared" majors. The closer students are to college, the more valuable the externship experience may be for getting day-in-the-life glimpses into a particular career or field of study.

BEGIN WITH THE END IN MIND: HOW TO SET UP SENIOR EXTERNSHIPS

Setting up a successful externship program requires knowing whether students (1) will create mentor-supported individual projects; (2) plan to return to their original internship placements; (3) seek new externship placements; or (4) some combination of the above.

Once these factors have been determined, it is important to consider the timeline for the experience. Keep in mind that the college application process is ongoing until at least December. It is thus a good idea to introduce the externship program at the beginning of the year and then come back to it as winter break gets closer. This gives students an opportunity to talk to potential mentors and their parents about ideas for externship over break. It also avoids overwhelming them with this task while they are focused on submitting college applications.

THE CADAVER LAB, A LIFE-ALTERING SENIOR CAPSTONE

"THE CADAVER LAB HELPED STUDENTS UNDERSTAND SOMETHING PROFOUND. IT WAS NO LONGER JUST ABOUT A LAB CLASS; THIS WAS HELPING HUMANITY."
—*Marilyn Rahlf, Capital Region Academies for the Next Economy (CRANE)*

Twelfth grade students arrived at the Medical Laboratory Sciences building at Folsom Lake College by bus. As a group they were quite diverse, comprised of various socioeconomic and cultural backgrounds and hailing from places as far as the mountain community of Placerville to the Central Sacramento Valley communities of Galt, West Sacramento, and Orangevale. What united them was their commitment to the Allied Health Pathway.

Sacramento County Office of Education's CRANE staff collaborated with Folsom Lake College's Pre-Health Alliance Club to offer students a full "college experience." The high school seniors met with college students in the Medical Laboratory Sciences program, learning firsthand about college classwork, extended university studies and possible careers. The experience culminated in a visit to the cadaver lab.

The students entered the lab and saw an open cadaver displayed on a table. Unlike the mannequins they had studied in their courses, this was the real body of an 80-year-old female who had died of cancer. A professor walked students through "quadrants" of the cadaver, explaining the location of organs and their function in the human body. For the students, who had only learned such information from books or small animal dissections, "this was an awe-inspiring experience," according to Marilyn Rahlf, CRANE career specialist. "To see 'real organs' as they fit inside the body was pretty surreal."

Students noticed there was still polish on the cadaver's fingernails. Rahlf notes that these details made the experience compelling for students. "They stopped seeing the body as a specimen," she said. "These were real people and that made a lasting impression on every student. They recognized that this is what medicine is all about, finding out about the person and how they died."

After the experience at the cadaver lab, students returned to their biomedical classes and continued to study human anatomy, now able to relate the material to what they had experienced. Some students who participated in the cadaver lab experience went on to intern at their local hospital.

Such experiences "expose [students] to careers they may not even know about, skills they don't know they have, and they give students a taste of reality of their potential futures," says CRANE career specialist Brandee Brewer. Both Brewer and Rahlf believe that partnerships like the cadaver lab provide lasting impact and create valuable opportunities for students that exist long after the initial experience. "Sometimes we are planting the seeds and we don't always hear the outcomes," Brewer notes. "But we know we are planting the seeds, and it's just a matter of time."

Consider the following timeline for rolling out an externship program:

FALL
Introduce students to the idea of externship and share the school's expectations for the experience. Up to this point, students may have done projects or engaged in curriculum that have been largely teacher-designed and featured increasing amounts of student input. However, the externship will be their capstone project-based learning experience. Their goal will be to design their own project with an outside mentor or co-design a project with a community partner organization.

EARLY JANUARY
Set time aside each week for student cohorts to work with teachers to identify where externships will take place and what the experience will look like for the student. Provide students with a list of externship requirements, frequently asked questions about project specs and deadlines and, where possible, a list of past internship and externship placements.

MID-JANUARY
This is a good time for students to pitch their project ideas for approval. Pitches should cover the 7Ps—purpose, perspective, product, plan, price, place, and presentation. It is ideal for teachers, the school director, the school dean, parents, and a community mentor to be present for the pitch. During the pitch, the student identifies her project and its timeline. All adult parties must sign off on the project pitch.

The key people involved in the externship experience are the student, the teacher, and the community mentor. In planning, consider the role of each of these stakeholders before, during, and after the externship experience.

THE STUDENT'S ROLE

BEFORE

At HTH, externship placements are solidified before spring break. This gives the few students whose externship falls through, or who cannot find one, extra time to secure an experience. The school break also allows students to start thinking in earnest about what their project work will be and how to connect with their mentors. When considering sites, students review a list of internship placements from past experiences and then reach out to potential contacts via email or phone. Remind students that they are expected to communicate professionally with potential mentors, and let them spend class time making these connections.

As they connect with professionals, encourage students to copy teachers on email inquires. This allows the teacher to help students reach out if they get no response; it also assures potential mentors that teachers are involved in this process. Copying teachers also serves an equity purpose: For those students whose families do not have community connections that could facilitate externship opportunities, the teacher is that connection. While the goal is to have students make these connections on their own, they are still in the process of learning how to do so. As 12th grade teacher Stephanie Lytle points out, "They are all coming from different steps to start with, so we can help them with that. We aren't doing it for them, we are just, as their teachers, helping them get started."

Next, students prepare an overview of what they will need for a project or what ideas they have for their work. If they are returning to a site at which they interned, a project is not necessarily required, but students should at least increase their responsibilities—they should not be doing the same tasks they did during internship. This is typically possible because most seniors are 18 by this point, and many companies will let them take on more responsibility. A good example of this comes from Chase, a senior at High Tech High International. For externship, Chase returned to the solar panel company where he had interned as a junior, where his experience consisted of creating visuals and web materials. He learned the ins and outs of the business, but got very little hands-on experience with solar panel installation and design. When he returned for externship, however, he worked with clients to create Google Sketchup designs of solar panel installations and was even part of the team that physically installed them.

Regardless of whether they have a new placement or are returning to a familiar site, all students undergo the design thinking process for an independent project. This allows them to think about how they could put their skills to work and who they could connect with in the community. They are encouraged to "dream big" as they work to make their project ideas reality.

DURING
Students typically complete their externship Monday to Friday for about 30 hours each week. This schedule can be adjusted depending on the organization's needs or operating hours.

Students can successfully document their experience by posting on social media, blogs, or video journals. Some teachers expect students to post daily; others set specific post quotas (such as posting at least three times per week, or making a post every Tuesday and Thursday). These posts may have specific requirements, such as being a certain length or including a picture or video, or perhaps responding to a prompt. Students also typically help facilitate site visits for their teacher, who usually makes two to three visits per student at times when the mentor is also available.

AFTER
Upon return from externship, all students present their learning to a cohort that may include teachers, students, mentors, school administrators, advisors, and parents. Finally, students send a handwritten note thanking their site mentor and anyone else who helped them accomplish their externship goals.

THE TEACHER'S ROLE

BEFORE

Many teachers launch externship by devoting a period a week to identifying externship goals and plans with students. One way to do this is to divide students into cohorts of about 20 by course or "profession." Re-imagine the schedule to carve out 30 to 60 minutes of the day (once a week or more) where, instead of attending core classes, students spend time with a faculty cohort leader. Students interested in externships that are focused on the arts and humanities would spend one hour of their day with their "cohort leader," one of the art or humanities teachers on campus; students interested in engineering could spend that hour with a physics or engineering teacher; and those students interested in biomedical sciences could spend that hour with a biology or chemistry teacher.

DURING

Successful externships are marked by significant teacher involvement. Teachers visit all externship sites within the first week to ensure that students and mentors are starting the experience well. After that, some teachers find it useful to maintain a "teacher blog," where they showcase their students' experiences. They might document the highlights of the externships and/or post examples of work they see students engaged in when they conduct site visits. Teachers also use this space to share examples of high quality student blog posts, so other students have models. This highlights what students are doing and keeps them connected to and motivated by their peers' activities. Other teachers in the school may also find it useful to consult the blog so they can keep up with what students in their advisory or homeroom are doing.

Teachers visit each student two to three times over the course of the externship. These visits are useful for helping students maintain good relationships with their mentors. Mentors especially appreciate these visits if they need encouragement, support, or ideas for how to work with students and/or give them more responsibility. Teachers can help students take professional-looking pictures of themselves at externship and help them think of ways to write about their experiences. In general, teachers are accessible and available to students for the duration of the externship.

AFTER

At the conclusion of the experience, teachers work with students to create a schedule for their externship presentation (ePOL). This involves pulling together student work samples, including their reflective pieces, and serves as a graduation portfolio that highlights their best work. Grant time for students to create their ePOL.

It is good practice for teachers to send mentors a digital survey to find out how the externship experience could be improved and if they would consider having an extern (or intern) another year; if so, be sure to add them to a database of possible future mentors. Finally, thank each mentor in writing for taking time to work with students. Writing such a note serves two purposes: it shows appreciation to the mentor for facilitating the externship experience and also maintains a relationship for future externships or project work.

THE COMMUNITY MENTOR'S ROLE

Successful externships are marked by significant mentor involvement.

BEFORE

Returning mentors who are already familiar with the program may have little to do to prepare for the externship, other than ensure the project is coherent and the workplace is ready for a high school student's presence. For new mentors, HTH teachers typically hold a site visit to observe the working space and answer any mentor questions. Students are typically present for this visit. Returning and new mentors are asked to discuss how students will spend their time; teachers can help with this process by reaching out via email or phone in advance.

At HTH, mentors (new and returning) are invited to a mentor lunch (or breakfast) so teachers can discuss with them expectations of the externship and have past mentors present their experiences and advice. For non-local mentors, these conversations can take place via Skype.

DURING

Mentors regularly review student blogs or reflections on the externship work and sign off on timesheets, if students are externing during the school day.

AFTER

Mentors fill out a survey about the experience and attend their mentee's externship presentation.

The hope for externship is that students will get valuable day-in-the-life experience in an industry they plan to study, or get an opportunity to try something they have never done before. This was Diego's experience. Diego completed a junior internship with an engineering firm, as he intended to one day become an engineer. But Diego was a funny student, always cracking a joke and getting laughs from those around him. Through the design thinking process initiated by his teachers to consider externship possibilities, Diego decided he wanted to try stand-up comedy. He reached out to several comedians in the area and finally, through the support of his teacher, found a mentor. His mentor put him in contact with a variety of experts and even helped him get on stage at a comedy show, which was the culminating externship experience. Diego went on to major in engineering in college, but he is also part of his university's comedy improv team. The externship process provided Diego an opportunity to pursue not necessarily a career path, but an endeavor that brought him joy. For students, the externship experience creates a way to more deeply understand their skills and interests, readying them for the next phase of their lives.

PROJECTS LEND THEMSELVES TO MULTIPLE FORMS OF ASSESSMENT, AND ASSESSMENT IS INFORMATIVE, REFLECTIVE AND COLLABORATIVE.

CHAPTER 5

STUDENT CENTERED ASSESSMENT

BY SARAH STRONG
HIGH TECH HIGH

ASSESSMENT FOR THE REAL WORLD

"Unless we rethink assessment, we will continue to educate the followers of yesterday rather than the leaders of tomorrow."

—*Eric Mazur*

How can assessment practices be designed to best support student learning? In school, the term "assessment" is often shorthand for "grades"—or, perhaps, tests, quizzes, rubrics, and similar evaluative tools. However, thinking of "assessment" as interchangeable with "test" or "grade" limits the potential for assessment practices to lead to meaningful and deeper learning.

Reforming classroom assessment starts by understanding that everyone is capable of valuable assessment and, in fact, does so all the time. When teachers make assessment practices transparent and invite students to participate in the process, they help students articulate what—and how—they are learning and what they most value in their education. Called student-centered assessment, this shift in perspective and practice brings meaningful activities into the classroom and sends important student work into the community.

Student-centered assessment requires that assessment is no longer something that happens to students via teacher-determined standards, grades, or non-negotiable tests. Rather, assessment becomes a set of practices that students apply to their work to understand and articulate what they find important and why. When done well, this type of assessment is subject to a variety of perspectives and provides a vehicle for equity: all classroom voices are heard and valued and all students are given opportunities find their strengths and growth areas. Student-centered assessment practices are informative, collaborative, and reflective.[1] These practices occur when students self-assess, peer-assess, when the teacher's role shifts, and when the classroom and school structure provide support for student participation—or even leadership—in assessment. While student-centered assessment occurs most seamlessly within the parameters of project-based classrooms, the practices can be incorporated into any classroom.

STUDENTS AS SELF-ASSESSORS

Student-centered assessment practices begin, somewhat naturally, with student self-assessment. When all students critically look at their own work and habits, and when their assessments are taken seriously, they are empowered to begin the work of projects, problem solving, and deeper learning. One step toward students developing agency over their own learning is discovering how to articulate—with examples and evidence—what matters to them. Why is this work important? What do we value in this work and why? What difference does this work make? Where is our work headed, in terms of our learning and our impact on the world? These questions lead to the broadening of assessment practices. No longer are narrow testing categories, or even teacher-prescribed expectations, enough. Instead, the rich world of student voice allows for more real-world assessment. It is in this opportunity for student voice that a path to equity can be forged. It is also in these conversations that students develop a greater sense of agency—value, belongingness, growth mindsets—as learners. We highlight practices that provide opportunities for student voice and, in turn, equity and agency: facilitating strengths-based self assessments, curating portfolios of student work, conducting presentations of learning, and facilitating student-led conferences.

SELF ASSESSMENTS: SHARING PERSONAL STRENGTHS

Students bring a wealth of strengths, skills, and preferences to the classroom. To facilitate thoughtful, personal self assessments in their classes, teachers need to help students acquire the language to describe their own strengths and to specifically call out their areas of growth. Before beginning a project or having students join a group, teachers should have students take stock of their personal strengths and growth areas. This helps them frame the work they are about to do, making the most of their strengths and making them able to share their strengths with their peers and teachers. These self-assessments help team members learn how to support one another, maximize complementary strengths, and mitigate potential conflicts.

Teachers can provide examples of strengths they feel relate to the work of their classroom and help students select a few to share with peers. Some teachers cut strips of different colored paper representing these strengths and place them at the front of the room, or across tables. Students come up and select two strips they feel most relate to them. They then bring the strips back to the table and share with their peers in a way that suggests they are "physically bringing their strengths to the table." Identifying and discussing the strengths they see in themselves helps students proceed through group work or partnerships more effectively and helps each student feel like they have a place. Examples of strengths might include:

- I am comfortable with uncertainty.

- I like to work persistently on challenging work.

- I can create convincing arguments.

- I like to find new solutions to old problems.

- I like to identify the moving parts of a complex situation.

- I like to organize large quantities of information.

- I like to simplify complex information.

- I like to help team members through a challenging task.

- I like to help people with different opinions peacefully reach consensus.

strengths finder

The National School Reform Faculty's "Compass Points" is another activity that helps students pinpoint their inherent strengths. Are some students quick actors who like to jump into new experiences ("Northerners")? Do some prefer to take a step back and look at the big picture ("Easterners")? Are some always aware of peers' emotions, and careful to include all voices ("Southerners")? Do some pay close attention to details ("Westerners")?[2] Once the directions are announced, students physically move to the part of the room they feel represents their personality. Once grouped according to compass points, they identify the strengths and challenges of their personality, and share their self-assessments with the class before joining a group to do work.

Regardless of the specific activity, students should regularly share their self-assessed strengths with each other and with their teachers. Sharing strengths aloud gives students' self-assessments explicit value in the classroom. By communicating these self-assessments to teachers and peers, students share valuable insights into their identities and needs, and offer opportunities to engage them more personally.

Self-assessing strengths, habits, and preferences powerfully sends the message that Elizabeth Cohen and Rachel Lotan identify in their research: "All of us have some of these abilities" and "None of us has all these abilities."[3] This is, at its heart, a message of equity; it empowers students who struggle to find their place in the classroom and reminds higher status students that they too have areas of growth.

SELF-ASSESSMENT USING MENTOR EXAMPLES

Another way to approach self-assessment is to offer students the opportunity to explain, with evidence, what they think of their work—and if a grade is on the line, to allow students to determine the parameters and values for themselves. This tool could be used at the start or middle of a project to help students articulate what constitutes beautiful work for that particular assignment or project. It could also be used at the end of a project as the criteria by which students assess final products.

Mentor examples—outstanding work done by professionals, peers, or other community members —help align student and teacher expectations regarding many aspects of project-based learning, and student self-assessments are no exception. Students compare

STUDENT

TEACHER

AUDIENCE

their work to a few high quality mentor examples and then answer two questions, being sure to include evidence from both the exemplary work and their own:[4]

1. How does your work measure up favorably to professional examples? Copy & paste samples of professional work (or use photos) and show how your work is similar to that of professionals.

2. How does your work need to grow, change, or improve to be more like that of professionals? Copy & paste samples of professional work (or use photos) and show how your work needs to grow, change, or improve in order to be more like that of professionals.

This type of self-assessment assumes that all students do some things well and all have room to grow. Those students who have historically struggled in class can be guided to build on their strengths (and to note that they are doing some things similar to professionals), and the students who feel that their first draft is good enough for an "A" must articulate areas in which they can continue to improve.

Self-assessing in the context of high quality examples helps teachers shift summative assessments to formative ones that address a student's ongoing growth. When students articulate what they value in professional work, they offer information about their own decision making and evaluative processes and provide valuable insight into how they see their own trajectory. The results of this practice help better align a teacher's work with what their students need and want.

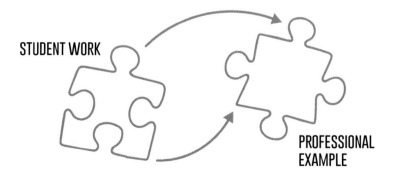

STUDENT WORK

PROFESSIONAL EXAMPLE

This protocol is designed to help students critique their work in the context of high quality examples and to craft an evidence-based response that assesses their successes and areas for continued growth. These evidence-based self-evaluations are useful in portfolio development, future reflections, and a variety of ongoing assessment practices.

FIRST : Students, get your work! As you complete this self-assessment, be sure to have the following easily available: your final draft of your work, the provided professional example, and another high quality example of similar work that influenced you.

THEN : Answer the following, and include direct evidence wherever necessary.

1. What are you most proud of in this project?

2. How does your work measure up favorably to professional examples? Copy & paste samples of professional work (or use photos) and show how your work is similar to that of professionals.

3. How does your work need to grow, change, or improve to be more like that of professionals? Copy & paste samples of professional work (or use photos) and show how your work needs to grow, change, or improve in order to be more like that of professionals.

4. What was the most effective feedback that you received while drafting and revising your work? Copy/paste the feedback below (or use photos) and describe with evidence how it influenced your subsequent work.

5. What questions do you have about how your ongoing work?

6. Overall, what are the most significant takeaways from thinking about your work in the context of high quality examples?

This protocol can also be used to have students grade their own work—if this is desired, simply add, "What grade would you award your work and why?" Then, use students' responses as an opportunity to align your vision of quality with theirs. You will gain insight into how and why they made project-related decisions and be better positioned to support them in creating work that is more finely tuned to professional standards that you—and, most importantly, the students—respect.[5]

ANALYZING PROFESSIONAL WORK IN THE LIBERTY RANCH HIGH SCHOOL AGRICULTURE PROGRAM

At Liberty Ranch High School, Mandy Garner engages her students in projects in the adult professional world through a variety of agricultural Career Technical Education classes: floriculture, advanced floral design, agriculture biology, agriculture leadership, and elements and principles of design. Her students run agricultural businesses—they provide floral services for weddings and formal events in the community, run a community-supported agriculture box program, and more. Mandy and her students regularly compare their work to professional examples because in many ways, it is their competition.

In the spring of 2016, Mandy began asking her students to provide written self-assessments of their work. Initially, this was an imperfect art, until she began requiring students to include photographs and detailed analyses of their professional influences. Mandy took similar self-assessments from English and history classes that asked students to compare their writing to professional writing. She adapted these to fit the needs of CTE classes; rather than have students use text-based quotations to compare their writing to professional examples, Mandy's students photograph examples of professional work similar to what they do in class, and compare them to their own work with corresponding evidence of their own processes and products. Now, as each student works on a project, he or she saves important photographs, plans, and related documents from his or her work, and similar elements from relevant professional work. As each student product is shared with adults in the community, either because it is sold via one of the school-run businesses, or because their work is regularly displayed in the school community, students speak and write in response to prompts like "My work is similar to professional work in that..." or "I am working to more like the professionals in that..."

PORTFOLIOS: THE POWER IN COLLECTED WORK

STUDENT-LED CONFERENCES

Student-curated portfolios are at the center of student-led conferences, which are dialogical, collaborative, formative forms of assessment, and a powerful way for students to take ownership over the traditional parent-teacher conference. In a student-led conference, the student guides a conversation about his or her strengths and areas of growth, and, importantly, takes the lead in selecting work samples from his or her portfolio. Throughout the conversation, the student provides an informative and reflective account of his or her progress and planned next steps; parents and teachers ask questions of and provide support for the student's assessments. For more on student-led conferences, please see Chapter 2.

SLCs can begin at the youngest grade levels in a school. "SLCs are kindergarteners' first experience talking about their learning," explained Cereescia Sandoval, a kindergarten teacher at High Tech Elementary. She went on to say, "Sometimes kids get the sense that they go to school to go to school and that they don't play a part in their learning. SLCs show them that they play a part in and are in control of their own learning." To set the kindergarteners up for success, the teacher and her aid sat with kids in groups of two or three. They discussed what was "already in their brains" and made a list of things they wanted to put in their brains. When they sat down with their parents and the teacher at the SLC, the students were comfortable with the language and practice of self-assessment and had work and pictures to use as evidence of their self-assessments.

PRESENTATIONS OF LEARNING

Similar to student-led conferences, portfolios provide the evidence for reflective presentations of learning, a rite of passage at the end of a term in which students address questions about growth towards, and mastery of, learning goals, academic mindsets, and deeper learning competencies. Importantly, students are empowered as self-assessors to select not only the work samples, but also to articulate answers to open-ended questions about the purpose of their work, their engagement in it, and their next steps beyond these experiences. Even formal records of student performance and notices to families are

PORTFOLIOS SHOW THAT I AM COLLEGE AND CAREER READY
JENN ISBELL, RESEARCH AND COMMUNICATION TEACHER

At Central Coast New Tech High School, students begin a portfolio project during ninth grade, in a Research and Communication class where they learn digital citizenship, begin their resume, and learn how to reflect in a structured way. The portfolio project is guided by the essential question, "How can I show that I am college and career ready?" Each student adds answers to this question, and more, to his or her personal website throughout the next three years. During their senior year English class, students prepare for their Defense of Learning, in which they share the portfolio of work they have curated over the years with an audience of teachers, parents, and friends. This is where they present the full answer to the question: "How can I show that I am college and career ready?"

"After watching the kids do these last year I am just blown away by the level of professionalism and the way that they command the audience," said Jenn Isbell, ninth grade Research and Communication teacher. "They have a very deep level of reflection, and they use this as an opportunity to talk about challenges and how they overcame the challenges and turned them into learning experiences where they grew. They are so self-aware and they are leaving with a renewed level of confidence saying 'Don't worry about me, I'm ready to head out into the world!'"

Portfolios, or collections of student work, provide a structured way for students to participate in evidence-based self-assessment over the course of a class, a year, or more. To develop a well-curated portfolio, students collect artifacts of their learning processes—drafts, critiques, and work samples—and organize them with written commentary that reflects their feelings, the process of completing the work, and its personal importance. Teachers should have students return to their portfolios as they wrap up the school year and reflect on the ways they have grown in content mastery, skills, and mindsets.

influenced by presentations of learning: these are opportunities for students to contribute to the written comments often included on report cards. For more on presentations of learning, see Chapter 2.

Both practices—student-led conferences and presentations of learning—offer the opportunity for students to evaluate:

- Their mastery of important learning goals and skills.
- Their growth and development within a specific context, grade level, or discipline.
- Their learning processes and habits.
- Their feeling about their work and educational experiences.
- Instructional methods that work well for them, and methods that challenge them.
- What they are most proud of and why.
- Goals and next steps.

STUDENT AS PEER ASSESSOR

"The fellow-pupil can help more than the master because he knows less. The difficulty we want him to explain is one he has recently met. The expert met it so long ago that he has forgotten. He sees the whole subject, by now, in such a different light that he cannot conceive what is really troubling the pupil; he sees a dozen other difficulties which ought to be troubling him but aren't." —CS Lewis as quoted in "Show your work!"[6] by Austin Kleon

As we step out from the students as individuals, we find them in a classroom of their peers who are an essential support system for shifting conventional roles of assessment. Students have the ability to assess other students in a way that teachers cannot: because students are members of a shared culture with their peers, they can frame feedback in ways that facilitate understanding differently than an adult would. And, when students are supported in identifying specific learning goals and practiced in providing critical feedback, they exponentially increase the instructional power of a single adult teacher. As a result, when given the right tools and scaffolds, formative assessment provided by peers can help each student create higher quality work than would have been possible otherwise.

Students can learn to meaningfully assess their peers through group work, peer critique, and classroom discussions that are supported with exit cards or feedback sheets—simple assessment tools that quickly provide valuable information to one another and teachers.

GROUP WORK & PEER ASSESSMENT

The design of many projects requires students to work together to produce something, and as they do, they have a close view of the processes of drafting, critique, and revision, as well as group dynamics and peer leadership. Naturally, students offer a valuable perspective when they assess their peers while working in groups.

The dynamics of group work vary from class to class; regardless, students can take on specific roles, specific tasks, or individual responsibility for a particular step. For many group tasks—especially ones in which the teacher hopes that all students will equally access similar content knowledge—teachers rotate roles among the group, such as:

- Facilitator: Ensures team excellence and equitable participation.

- Reporter: Collects notes and data about the work and shares with the group and class.

- Questioner: Asks and answers questions among the group and involves the teacher only when the group is truly "stuck."

- Production Manager: Maintains team or class materials and supplies, and assists in day-to-day task management.

Other teachers give specific jobs to students for the duration of the project (i.e., director, cinematographer, audio tech, etc.). Within these roles, the teacher and group works together to assure that the work for the project is spread appropriately among each person in the group.

Following group tasks, exit cards provide an efficient way to evaluate the student experience, and for the student to provide evaluative feedback about their experience. Distribute an index card to each student, and have them respond to two or three of the following prompts:

1. Describe what went well for you today.
2. Describe how your team worked well today.
3. Describe what you learned today.
4. What could have been better about class today?
5. What has been challenging for you? Why?
6. What has been challenging for your team? Why?
7. What do you or your group need to make progress tomorrow?

after labs?

Exit cards give the teacher information from students about their dynamic experiences in class, and that information helps the teacher decide among next steps: should students continue doing the type of activities that they previous did? Are group structures working well? Should specific students receive feedback about their progress on the project or group interactions? Do students need a restorative conversationn or intervention? Is there exemplary work, behavior, or insightful feedback that should be shared with the class?

Outside of open-ended exit cards, some teachers will ask students to list specific accomplishments and challenges according to their responsibilities within the group: what tasks did they get done and what still needs to be done? Other teachers use exit cards aligned to specific learning goals in class or project tasks. Regardless of the format, students' daily assessments provide feedback to the teacher, their peers, and for themselves. Group roles and exit cards lead to entry points and accountability for each person in the group; each student feels a unique responsibility and commits to the work of assessing and supporting his or her peers.

Regardless of the group structure or the peer assessments, groups do not receive group grades. Ultimately, teachers and individual students establish individual grades based on the feedback that they collect about their work and their personal assessment of this feedback. The goal is to leverage student perspectives for valuable information and support, not to allow a whole group to be labelled as a "B+".

PEER CRITIQUE: FORMATIVE PEER ASSESSMENT

Peer critique offers unique opportunities for peer-to-peer assessment of important work samples. Peer critique comes in many shapes and sizes: the whole class may critique an individual example, individual students may critique specific work samples, or other arrangements in between (for more on specific critique practices, see Chapter 3).

For assessment purposes, during peer critiques students document the following on feedback sheets that they share with peers and teachers:

- Positive commentary that identifies strengths within the work.

- Kind, specific, and helpful suggestions for revision that are aligned to learning goals and project expectations.

- Potential mechanisms, data points, quotations, or pieces of evidence that can be used for ongoing assessment tools. Early critiques can inform rubric creation and later critiques provide evidence for students to show growth and/or mastery.

Holistically, peer critique offers valuable formative assessments of student progress that inform teachers' decision making: peer critique surfaces common next steps (these students should move on to the next step, but those need one more revision) and clusters categories of concern (too many students are struggling with this learning goal—let's slow down). Like self-assessments of work samples, peer assessment feedback sheets are saved in portfolios and used in student-led conferences, presentations of learning, or exhibitions of learning. Importantly, peer critique provides students the opportunity to hear formative feedback from peers, and to present their work to a relevant test audience to better understand how it will be perceived in a formal presentation, at exhibition of learning, or as a final product.

CLASSROOM DISCUSSION

Classroom discussions offer many opportunities to assess students' content knowledge, participation skills, and learning processes. Teachers and students can offer feedback on one another's statements, students can ask and answer questions to gather more information, and students can think aloud to try out new ideas and evaluate their validity. In good discussions both teachers and students recognize strengths and areas of growth in themselves and the classroom community.

Classroom discussions offer the opportunity to provide feedback that impact student learning because the observations, or even evaluations, are personal and happen quickly. During or after a discussion, teachers and students should use exit cards or feedback sheets that ask to address one or more of the following ideas:

- What was the most helpful aspect of today's discussion?

- What was the most valuable idea that you heard in the discussion today?

- What question(s) most helped you understand this work more deeply? Why?

- Did you change your mind about anything during the discussion? How & why?

- What was the most valuable contribution that you made to a peer, or the class as a whole, through this discussion?

- What do you think should be done differently in our next discussion?

Similar to exit cards used for peer assessment of group roles, exit cards or feedback sheets following classroom discussions can provide important information about student experiences. The possibilities for questions are endless—the power comes in identifying key pieces of information that inform the teacher's, and students', next steps.

STUDENT ROLES FOR CLASS DISCUSSIONS

In classes that feature regular discussion, student ownership of discussion roles provides opportunities to offer formative feedback of the many ways that students can contribute. In student-led discussions, roles may include:

- Discussion Leader or Facilitator
- Scribe or Reporter(s)
- Questioner(s)
- Discussion Participants

To flip the traditional, teacher-led class discussion of specific academic content, consider the following structure that uses the roles listed above: a prompt, problem set, text sample, or other artifact is shared with the students and they are given a set amount of time to think quietly at their desks about the content and make notes about what they notice and wonder. After students share ideas quickly at their tables, a few students move about the room to facilitate the class discussion (students with roles like "Discussion Leader" and "Scribe" may need to stand at the front of class or be positioned near whiteboards). The discussion leader prompts the class—this can be as general as "what ideas do we have about this picture?" and the scribe records the ideas that are shared. Or, the class may try to answer an essential question that the teacher provides or is inherent in the content at hand. At key points in the discussion, the teacher or Discussion Leader pauses the class and students share feedback on what their peers are doing well within the context of their roles:

- How well is the Discussion Leader integrating the whole class into the conversation?
- To what extent are the Scribe's notes useful to the class?
- How are the Questioners helping to uncover new ideas?
- To what extent is the class participating?

This can be done a variety of ways: pair-share (turn and talk with a neighboring student), feedback sheets with prepared questions, an open class discussion—or any combination of the three. Rich feedback ensues when these assessments also address the nature of the roles; the assessment of today's classroom discussion helps collectively define those roles and shares this information publicly with the class. From this, students learn to offer helpful peer-to-peer feedback about how they participated in the class discussion: whether they offered questions, ideas, or built on someone else's ideas. Importantly, this is a peer assessment of participation as a class member and is not content based.

SOCRATIC SEMINARS

The Socratic seminar is a widely used structure for classroom discussion that promotes useful peer assessment. In a Socratic seminar, the class is arranged with an inner and outer circle, and the students on the inner and outer parts of the circle are partnered. Before the discussion begins, each partner in the inner circle talks to his or her partner in the outer circle and records his or her goals on a feedback sheet held by the partner in the outer circle. The inner circle then has a discussion, and, the outer circle of partners listens to their discussion and records the contributions of their inner circle partners. Together, they decide if the partner in the inner circle is meeting his or her goals for the day. At the end of the discussion, the partners in the outer circle gives the feedback sheet back to their partner and they discuss his or her assessment—it can be valuable for both to write a quick reflection about what they learned based on how they approached their roles in the seminar. Students keep the feedback sheets and their reflections on each in a Socratic seminar journal that documents evidence of their growth.

A note about offering points for participation in classroom discussions: simply offering credit for vocal participation can negatively impact the richness of class discussions:
Some students—particularly those with higher social status or those highly concerned with grades—may monopolize the conversation in order to get the most participation points.
Some students may choose to stop participating once they reach an established amount of points. For example, if a teacher says that everyone must ask one question and offer one reference to the text, some students will ask a question that includes a reference to the text, and then tune out, as they have met the requirements.
Students who struggle to speak in class—especially English language learners or students in special education programs—may determine that they simply cannot succeed in this class.

Assessment systems that award credit for participation in classroom discussions need to be flexible, and incentivize a wide range of constructive participation.

SOCRATIC SEMINARS: INDIVIDUAL AND CLASS ASSESSMENTS FOR GROWTH
MARK AGUIRRE, HUMANITIES, HIGH TECH HIGH

Mark Aguirre uses Socratic seminars regularly in his Humanities class at High Tech High. For him, the seminars are formative assessment tools telling him how students are progressing on the things that he values in the class. "When I think of assessments, I think of individual growth and I think of class growth," stated Aguirre. At the end of each seminar, a librarian takes notes about what was talked about and they collectively decide what they can improve for next time. For example, one week the group decided they needed to talk about the text more and make sure that a few people do not monopolize the conversation. Mark explained, "Then we start the next session with the notes from the previous session to keep the collective classroom work moving forward."

THE TEACHER AS REFLECTOR: THE SHIFTING ROLE OF THE TEACHER IN STUDENT CENTERED ASSESSMENT

With the student at the center of assessment practices, the role of the teacher pivots. By design, in the project-based classroom and within student-centered assessment practices, the teacher is—literally and figuratively—not always found at the front of the classroom. By moving away from the whiteboard and podium, the teacher moves toward the role of collaborator. In this shift, the teacher engages students in authentic dialogue that emphasize growth and next steps. Specific practices that support this shifting role of the teacher are: one-on-one check-ins, co-created rubrics, and flipping the traditional test-based classroom.

Brian Delgado, a veteran science teacher at High Tech High, stated simply, "Assessment is a feedback loop with the purpose of improving performance and quality of work. Teaching and learning is the conversation." He went on to share that there are times when student work is submitted digitally through email or Google classroom, but these are just variations on the ongoing conversation in the classroom.

ONE-ON-ONE CHECK-INS

Perhaps the most under-noticed, intuitive, and all-around valuable form of assessment in the school is dialogue. One-on-one check-ins between a teacher and student are as much art as science and tend to serve three purposes: to build rapport, clarify one's thinking and habits, and to set learning goals together. One-on-one check-ins help students assess their work, recognize and share their progress toward goals, check their understanding, surface their approach or mindset, and come up with what to do next.

Check-in questions come in two varieties: open ended questions in which the student arrives at the answer, or leading questions, in which the teacher embeds his or her answer in the question (in the tuning protocol in Chapter 1, this is called "advice in disguise" and often sounds like "Don't you think you should..." or "Have you considered..."). Open ended questions ensure student-led assessment; leading questions are teacher centered. Early users may want to throw out the rules and just "fix" the problem. Unfortunately, if the result of a one-on-one check-in is the teacher telling the student the solution (and not the student setting goals), there is less likelihood of follow through or lasting ownership on the student's part.

When teachers and students have one-on-one check ins about the big picture of a student's experience in a class or within a discipline, consider questions such as:

- What are your goals for the semester/this project/your internship/etc?

- How would you describe yourself as a learner?

- Do you believe that if you work hard you will succeed in this class? Why?

- How can I help you get the most out of the work in this class?

- How can I help you really challenge yourself in this class?

Look for patterns in the students' answers. How might specific students need support in specific academic areas versus other factors such as maintaining growth mindset? What patterns do you notice in your class as a whole?

When teachers and students have one-on-one check ins about specific experiences within a project, or specific work samples, consider questions such as:

- How are you are doing?

- Can you show me how you are doing, with work from your portfolio?

- How many times have tried this? Or: how many drafts have you done?

- How are you making decisions in what to do next or when to stop?

Teachers (or students) record quotes and ideas from one-on-one check-ins in a spreadsheet to be revisited throughout the project or even the semester. When this practice is used for goal-setting, it is prudent to use the same spreadsheet and return to these goals during a mid-year check-in and then again at the end of the year. During subsequent check-ins, the students should provide evidence of movement toward these goals and/or revise the goals and add new ones. In complex projects, this spreadsheet helps track progress and helps the teacher determine who needs help and how. Towards the end of a semester, this spreadsheet contains valuable information to share with students and parents via written comments as an accompaniment to the end-of-semester grade. Such reports—or even simply copying the content for each student from the spreadsheet and sending it to families—provide deeper insights than letter grades into what the student knows and values, and what they hope to learn.

CO-CREATED RUBRICS

Another facet of the teacher's shifting role in student-centered assessment is the co-creation of rubrics with students. The purpose of this practice is to support the students in articulating what quality work looks like; their words and observations become the criteria for self-assessment, peer-assessment, and teacher assessments.

To begin the co-creation process, the teacher selects an example of what he or she considers to be high quality work—the teacher's expertise is in having developed a trained eye to identify inspiring examples of real-world work aligned with students' learning targets. Mentor example could come from professional work, a teacher-created example, or student created examples.

Co-creating a rubric from a mentor example can be time consuming, and for teachers who teach multiple class periods per day, it may seem overwhelming. There are several ways to resolve this:

- Give space for the class to analyze mentor example and identify what makes it great.

- Allow students to propose categories and language to help identify and describe aspects of high quality work.

- As students share categories and criteria, document their thoughts on a whiteboard, computer projected onto a screen, poster, or other easily visible part of the classroom.

- Help students organize their ideas as the discussion moves along. Mark ideas that come up more than once with a star or tally.

- At first, strive for a co-created checklist, not a complete rubric. A checklist is a valuable tool because it contains objective criteria of high-quality work, as articulated by students (i.e., students may state that articles must be 750 words and contain a headline, subhead, and two pull quotes; or, that engineering groups must interview three users and use specific technologies). A checklist is a good first step because it allows the students to say, "these are the things we see in great work," without having to determine all of the categories or values in a fully developed rubric.

- If (or, when!) students dissent or otherwise disagree with the ideas that are included in this process, save this information for future critiques or other assessment tools. These students may be probing for what constitutes honors credit, how to tailor work to their strengths, or expressing concerns about areas of growth that may need to be addressed.

For more information on co-created rubrics, see Chapter 3.

FLIPPING THE TRADITIONAL TEST-BASED CLASSROOM

While many of the practices in this section involve a complete pivot from the traditional teacher-centered and test-based classroom, it should be acknowledged that thoughtfully administered tests can have a place in student-centered assessment practices. For many (especially older) students, tests feel as "real life" as anything else. They see SAT's, ACT's, college placement tests, and many other high stakes tests on the horizon as gatekeepers to their future. These feelings should not be overlooked; rather, teachers can take this opportunity to engage students in conversations about the reasons behind traditional test construction, the necessities of scoring, and the nature of the testing genre itself, to help students when they face them. Having these discussions while giving students opportunities to practice test taking skills in a less stressful and non-judgemental space can help identify areas of growth—and address issues related to mastery of content knowledge.

GROUP TESTS

Collaborative or cooperative test-taking—allowing students to engage with tests in groups or partnerships—can refocus the test-taking experience on student learning. This can be implemented in a variety of ways:

- Distribute the test and allow a specified period of time for individual work. When that time is up, the students join together with a predetermined group to analyze the test items and discuss ideas, thoughts, and possible answers. The teacher might assign certain problems to certain groups of students and direct them to converge on an answer to share with the class (along with a justification) after a set amount of work time.

- Distribute the test to students in randomly assigned partnerships. Allow the students to work together on the test and when they are done, instruct them to answer reflective questions such as:

  - How did I help my partner?
  - How did my partner help me?
  - Did my partner lead me to change my mind on anything on the test? How/why?
  - If I work with this partner again, what might I do differently?

One important caveat: do not allow students to to choose their own partners in collaborative test-taking—the power lies in bringing every student up to a high standard, and self-selection of partners will undermine the goal of collective success.

NOT GRADING OR RECORDING THE TEST

One way to take the stress out of a test is to simply remove the grade from it all together. Students should take the test, score it together as a class, and then make an individual plan for improvement based on the performance on the test. This practice assumes that structures are set up in the class for the students to find value in a test that is not graded; if the class is built around project-based assessments like exhibitions and presentations of learning, then the test becomes just another part of the learning and practice needed to succeed in those contexts. And, as previously mentioned, at least for high schoolers, tests feel like a part of their real life. Framing the test as an important indicator of progress for a big class-wide exhibition or presentation of learning will reduce test-anxiety, yet put the onus on the student to do well on the test because it is an important step towards what is "real life," "important," or "authentic" to them: completing a project, performing well at a presentation, or having high-quality work to display at an exhibition.

ANNOTATING THE TEST

Another shift on the traditional test is to frame the test as a conversation piece between the teacher and students. Doing this shifts the test from a high stakes summative evaluation to another piece of the students' learning journey. In this type of test, the teacher provides prompts for the student to respond to as they work. For example, a teacher might format the test so that:

- There is area in the margin for the students to record thoughts, questions, or observations as they complete the test.

- There is room after each test item for the student to leave similar notes or feedback (thoughts, questions, observations).

- Each test item also includes a Likert scale (strongly agree to strongly disagree), or picture-based version, for students to indicate their confidence in their answers.

- The test includes instructions or the students to annotate the test items as they please with notes to the teacher—the teacher then assesses the student performance in the test and the types of notes he or she provided.

Student participation in an annotated test is meant to cultivate metacognition and provide insights to the teacher and to the student as they work. Students might share things like:

- The phrasing of this question was confusing to me.

- This is not a word that I am familiar with.

- I feel very strong on problems like this.

- I am comfortable with the material, but this was a new type of question that I haven't seen before.

ALLOW STUDENTS TO RETAKE TESTS

The idea that all students should know the same thing at the same time is outdated and unrealistic. Allowing students to be a part of the conversation that people learn things at different rates, different depths, and different times frees them from the stress of a seemingly all-powerful summative assessment that is taken, graded, and never looked at again. When a student retakes a test, he or she transforms it from a summative assessment to a formative one. When teachers allow for re-do's, they create new categories of important information to assess: did you retake that test, and why or why not? Allowing students to re-do their tests sends the message that learning doesn't ever end, and that mistakes—even on a test—aren't the end, but rather an opportunity for growth.

THE CULTURE OF THE CLASSROOM AND SCHOOL

While self-assessment, peer-assessment, and shifting teachers' roles will transform assessment for students, they will also impact classroom and school culture—which in turn can impact their effectiveness as processes that put the student at the center of assessment practices. Classroom and schoolwide practices that sustain student-centered assessment include exhibitions of student learning, assessments of school-wide student perception data, the use of digital portfolios, and the impacts of regularly held student-led conferences and presentations of learning.

EXHIBITION

Just before an exhibition of learning, the school buzzes with students putting finishing touches on displays, sprucing up classrooms, preparing speeches and performances, and hanging final products on walls and in hallways. Parents, teachers, outside experts, and other community members gather to see the work that the students have worked on all semester long. Ideally, an exhibition of learning is built into the project, class, or even school structure and is an authentic assessment of the students' work and learning. Although this is an assessment, there is minimal grading or scoring of students at an HTH exhibition, and grades are not the motivating factor to do well at an exhibition of learning. Because students know that visitors are coming to see what they wrote, built, or created, they prepare their work to be at the highest quality and prepare to speak articulately about their learning in the process.

To prepare for an exhibition of learning, teachers and students use self-assessments and peer assessments of specific elements of the exhibition event. To prepare for an open-house, gallery-style exhibition, students should quiz each other with lists of possible questions visitors might ask. They can do this in small groups, or by taking volunteer students to take questions in front of the class. For an exhibition event that involves public speaking, students should draft, critique, and revise their speeches as they would with any other element of project work—and they should save artifacts of these peer assessments to surface all that they have learned throughout the project.

During or following an exhibition of learning, seek feedback from students and the guests who visit the school via exit cards. Consider prompts or questions such as:
- At this exhibition of learning, I learned...
- One element of exhibition that struck me was...
- I wondered about...

TRANSFORMING OPEN HOUSE THROUGH EXHIBITION
JOSH KRISTOFF, MATH TEACHER
ACADEMY OF THE CANYONS MIDDLE COLLEGE HIGH SCHOOL

Joshua Kristoff, a math teacher at Academy of the Canyons Middle College High School, helped transition his school's traditional open house evening event into an exhibition of student learning to provide a more real-world assessment of work.

At the newly-minted exhibition of student learning, Josh's students displayed storyboards of an original motion picture. They created scenes and also the storyline that goes along with it and incorporated math and English via the process of making an animated film. Josh reflected, "As we head into an age where we don't know what the world is going to look like, students will need to be able to learn and unlearn quickly. This means that the information you have isn't always relevant and so you need to be able to flexibly learn a new way or technique to do things." Rather than assess students only on a set of mathematical equations that they may or may not recall for a test, Josh was interested in what they articulated about their learning processes.

Josh felt the event was a success, stating, "The purpose of the exhibition evening is to get students to display authentic projects. In the past, similar open house events were traditionally a parent night where students came if they wanted to get extra credit. It was very rarely student-centered. Now we want to focus on the students' work, showing both the product and the process and both are very important. We want students to feel comfortable talking about what they made and the process of how they made it. Exhibition is the ultimate form of assessment because not only are we able to assess the product, but the process. If they have the ability to articulate what happened at the beginning, middle, and end, it helps students think about learning—and not just about the content, but learning about their learning."

SCHOOLWIDE DATA COLLECTION: DATA, WELL-BEING, AND MINDSETS

The school can also set the tone for student-centered assessment practices by thoughtfully selecting the type of data that is collected and shared among teachers, students, and parents. While traditional state tests are often used as the measure of a school, increasingly schools are using surveys to assess student perceptions in categories like academic rigor, relationships with teachers, college and career readiness, and relevance of curriculum. School administrators should set aside staff meetings to unpack the this type of data and have teachers collaboratively identify actionable goals in areas of deficit and in maximizing strengths. Large, nationally-normed surveys exist, such as YouthTruth, but if the school, or perhaps a small group of teachers, cannot join such a project, they can create one of their own by using free survey software online. Consider Likert-scale style surveys with prompts such as:

- I can succeed in school by working hard.

- My success in school is directly connected to my effort.

- The work I do in school is relevant to my life outside of school.

- My teachers understand me well as a student.

- My teachers understand who I am as a person in and out of school.

- I am learning to collaborate well at school.

- I am learning to communicate effectively at school.

- I am learning how to learn at school.

Individual teachers can assess student perceptions at any point in the school year. Any teacher can use the questions listed above by changing the language from "at school" to "in this class." Or, a teacher may offer open-ended questions such as:

- How is your project work in this class relevant to your life inside or outside of school?

- Describe times when you had to work hard in this class.

- Describe a time when you felt supported by your teacher in this class.

- Describe a time when you felt like you needed more support in this class.

Teachers can unpack answers to these questions alone or in small groups with colleagues, depending on their preferences. Importantly, teachers should select relevant portions of the survey feedback and share these results with their students. One format that works well is to categorize elements of student feedback to celebrate, areas to grow, and questions, and share this with their classes. By doing this, teachers model an appropriate use of this assessment tool, and they can then make shifts to their practice to ensure they are attending to the needs of all of their students—and their shifts will be more likely to be understood by their students as part of a culture of ongoing assessment and improvement.

DIGITAL PORTFOLIOS

Digital portfolios are a structure that allow students to post their project work, reflect on the process, and broadly share this work in only a few clicks on a computer or a smartphone. Much like the portfolio work discussed in the self-assessment section above, digital portfolios are online sites that students create using personal website platforms or academically and professionally-focused social networks. After a project or unit ends, the students take their portfolio work samples, reflections, pictures, and links to final products and curate them in a digital space. In this process, students are first assessing themselves and their work throughout the semester; they then share their sites with their peers and teachers for further assessment. As a final step, students' digital portfolios may even be used as an assessment from colleges and universities as part of the admissions process.

THE IMPACT OF EXHIBITIONS OF LEARNING, STUDENT-LED CONFERENCES & PRESENTATIONS OF LEARNING

Schools that have shifted toward more student-centered practices have a decidedly different calendar. Instead of events like "finals week" and "parent-teacher conferences" bookending the semesters, the calendar would feature "Exhibition Night," "POL week" and "Student Led Conferences." The families and students prepare for and frame their year around these events and this creates a schoolwide message that these student-centered assessments are the culminating events, as opposed to a big test—and the school sends the message that all assessment is formative, as students continue to move to the next presentation, and next project, in their lives.

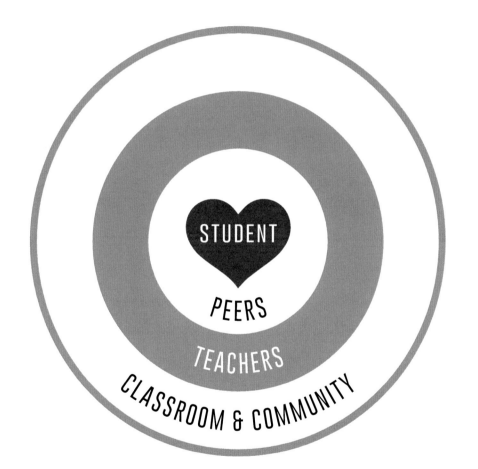

STUDENT

PEERS

TEACHERS

CLASSROOM & COMMUNITY

STUDENT-CENTERED ASSESSMENT IS ASSESSMENT FOR THE REAL WORLD

The more any quantitative social indicator is used for social decision-making, the more subject it will be to corruption pressures and the more apt it will be to distort and corrupt the social processes it is intended to monitor.

—Campbell's Law

Placing students at the center of assessment brings about a host of practices that increase students' reflective and collaborative skills, pivots the role of the teacher in the classroom, and can be enhanced by classroom and schoolwide structures. As we move from a school system designed for the industrial age to one designed for the global information age, we have to ask, "What do we value in school and why?" This questions begs others: Do we want to engage in practices that seem to value learning inert knowledge to pass a test and subsequently forgetting? Do we want to assess only a narrow band of skills and content with limited methods? Should the term "assessment" continue to be shorthand for "grades" and "tests"?

Student centered assessment is ultimately focused on cultivating students' abilities to learn how to learn. These are students who are recognized in internships and in the workplace, and move on to college as students who operate independently, yet know when to check in to ask questions and seek support. Producing students with these capacities is at the forefront of this work—upending the assessment system and placing students at the center is the first step to aligning our work with our hopes for what lies beyond school: the "real world."

REFLECTIVE PRACTICES FOSTER CYCLES OF INQUIRY AND FRAME
THE CULTURE AND VALUES OF THE SCHOOL AND COMMUNITY.

CHAPTER 6

REFLECTION

BY PETER JANA
HIGH TECH HIGH

TRANSFORM EXPERIENCE INTO MEANING

"True reflection leads to action. on the other hand, when the situation calls for action, that action will constitute an authentic praxis only if its consequences become the object of critical reflection."

—*Paolo Freire*

Self-understanding is one of the oldest and most venerated forms of wisdom; but it does not come easily. A figure no less than Socrates made it his lifelong quest and only managed to succeed in knowing what he did not know. When the Delphic Oracle implores us to "know thyself" or when Socrates informs us that the "unexamined life is not worth living," they are making the case for reflective learning as a lifelong process which is grounded in experience. For Socrates, this experience primarily involved dialectical conversations about the nature of truth, beauty, and virtue. For John Dewey in the twentieth century, it involved connecting personal experience to a larger educational and civic context. For both, reflection is the essential ingredient for life-long learning and personal growth. It transforms individual raw experience into personal meaning and collective value.

WHAT IS REFLECTION?

Reflection occurs when students and teachers think about what they are doing, why they are doing it, and what they have learned. It is the lynchpin of project-based learning (PBL) and the constructivist practices outlined in this book. At its most advanced, it is not simply the mind noticing what the hands are doing; it is a metacognitive endeavour of learning how the hands and mind work together and inform one another.

Metacognition is thinking about thinking with the aim of improving learning.[1] It occurs when a person evaluates his or her thinking and takes steps to understand and improve his or her thought patterns. A student who turns off her computer because she realizes that she is distracted by it, thinks metacognitively, as does a reader who can't understand a dense paragraph and consciously employs reading strategies to work through it.

WHY REFLECT?

Reflection is the pause in activity that allows students to think metacognitively and to make connections to other experiences and to evaluate what they learned. As recent neuroscience has shown, such pauses are essential for learning; in the words of Mary Helen Yang-Immordino, "rest is not idleness."[2] Taking a moment to reflect or event to simply rest increases the overall effectiveness of brain processing.[3] Similarly, planning for reflective opportunities at key moments in the curriculum allows for the "active retrieval" of past knowledge that assists in retention and creative thinking.[4]

As opposed to "one size fits all" assessments that often leave students behind, reflection promotes equitable access to deeper learning opportunities and outcomes. Facilitating structured time and space for individuals to think about their own thinking provides a diverse range of students with the opportunity to draw personal connections to the project, determine its relevance for their lives, and assess their individual strengths and challenges.

WHEN SHOULD IT HAPPEN?

Education involves a process of becoming—in the present we reflect on our past in order to project ourselves into the future. In PBL we can apply this principle by planning for reflection before, during, and after specific project components. These types of reflections can take the following forms:

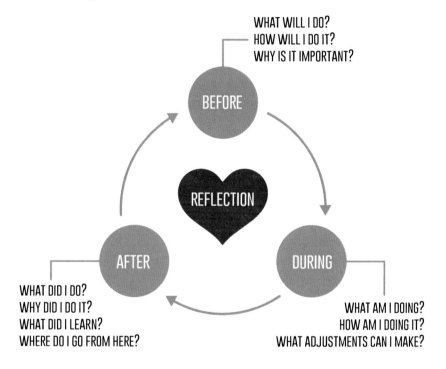

WHAT WILL I DO?
HOW WILL I DO IT?
WHY IS IT IMPORTANT?

BEFORE

REFLECTION

AFTER

DURING

WHAT DID I DO?
WHY DID I DO IT?
WHAT DID I LEARN?
WHERE DO I GO FROM HERE?

WHAT AM I DOING?
HOW AM I DOING IT?
WHAT ADJUSTMENTS CAN I MAKE?

The following offer prime opportunities for reflection at HTH and other schools that engage in PBL:

- Culminating events: exhibitions of learning, presentations of learning, student-led conferences, completing a major project, completing an internship.

- Transition in a student's academic life: advancing to another grade or graduating.

- Throughout project processes, including framing or designing a project, discovery, research, building, tuning, exhibition, assessment and debrief.

WHAT DOES REFLECTION LOOK LIKE IN THE CLASSROOM?

Students can reflect in writing that is shared with the teacher, students, the public, or is kept private. Common written forms of reflection:

- Exit cards
- Journaling
- Quick writes in which students make predictions, summarize, or ask questions, especially about their own thought processes
- Providing written feedback to the teacher about the lesson
- Self evaluations of important processes or procedures in class.
- Project evaluations

Students can reflect through small or large group discussion. Common forms of dialogic reflection structures:

- Pair share
- Walk and talk
- Proactive circles
- Reflective protocols
- Critique processes
- Project tunings

Teachers can reflect with their students by:

- Modelling metacognition through think aloud activities
- Modeling presentations (e.g. presentations of learning)
- Modeling and engaging in critique
- Working transparently with student feedback about projects or lessons
- Collaborative design

SMALL AND BIG REFLECTION

Reflection can also be "small" or "big" in nature. "Small reflection" is short, quick, and frequently impromptu. "Big reflection" is planned carefully and often part of the finished product, or during specific time set aside during key steps in the process of creating a project. While big reflection necessitates planning, using small reflection necessitates spontaneity. Big reflection requires teachers to plan for reflection like any other component of their project: teachers will want to consider how their project is mapped out and where students could most benefit from moments of analyzing their own thoughts. Small reflection, on the other hand, calls for teachers to be aware of moments, sometimes critical ones in projects, when students will benefit from the time to analyze, critique, or thoughtfully evaluate what is happening then and there.

Small reflection is helpful in the following circumstances:

- When unforeseen events occur, having students observe and document their thoughts about those events helps students see how those events are relevant to their personal and academic lives.

- When social problems arise, prompts that require students to share their recollection of what happened, what they were thinking at the time, who was impacted, and what they have thought about since the problem, helps students understand the cause of such problems and take steps towards reconciliation.

- When students say that they are "stuck," metacognitive prompts that lead them to analyze these thoughts help them get unstuck.

SMALL REFLECTION QUESTIONS

"Go-To" Questions

Working with students can, at any point, require moments to slow down and think about things. it is helpful to have a set of "Go-to" reflective questions or prompts ready for a variety of situations. These questions are effective when students need to self assess and to take a moment for reflection:

- What is going well? Why are these things going well?
- What could be improved? How am I thinking about these improvements?
- What next steps may be possible? What are my next steps?

"Gots and Needs" Questions

Teachers need to know where students are in their understanding. What did students "get" from a learning experience, and what do they "need" to keep making progress? Knowing when to move on or when the topic is difficult requires reflection for understanding to occur; "Gots and Needs" questions can help.

- What did I get from class today? What do I understand?

- What do I need to keep making progress? What don't I understand or what can't I access?

- What do I need now and how can I get it? What are my next steps?

Big reflection is helpful in the following circumstances:

- When the work spans a long period of time.

- When reflective moments occur at multiple and predictable points in time.

- In collections of work kept over time used to demonstrate growth.

- To determine if work is complete in order to move on in projects.

- To reflect on the work-to-date at key points in projects.

- To develop and maintain a rigorous analysis and clear articulation of the project's development for exhibitions of learning.

BIG REFLECTION QUESTIONS

Individual Portfolio Questions:

Many schools will keep portfolios (collections of student work) which allow students to select, keep, organize, and analyze samples of their work as evidence of their learning over long periods of time. Through reflection, this work can be used to help students understand their thought patterns and processes, and understand their growth.

- How has my work changed over time?
- What processes, procedures and/or resources account for the most significant changes in my work?
- How has my thinking changed over time in this subject/discipline?
- What specific pieces of my work are clear evidence of my growth or improvement?
- In what areas do I feel improvement is needed? Why do I say this?

Reflective questions can also be used to facilitate group work. Before student groups commence working, teachers should ask the group members to collectively determine their goals for the day, or even ask for a group leader or project manager to set goals and share them with his or her partners. Individuals within those groups should then set a plan for how they will help the group accomplish those goals. Teachers and students should set check in points—perhaps half-way through a class period, or at the end of specified amount of time, for teachers to prompt groups to pause and reflect on the progress they have made in the project. This will help the group determine whether it needs to continue or change course and do things differently. Keeping track of these reflections along with student work samples helps students clearly articulate how they did their work, how they made important decisions, how they communicated within the group, and what their thoughts are about these experiences.

These questions are effective in the course of group projects:

- How have I contributed to the work we have done to date?

- How have I documented what we have done so far?

- What can I learn from the work done so far? How can it help now in moving us forward?

- How is my thinking impacted by my group members?

- How have my thoughts had an impact on our group?

- Based on what we have done so far, what is our next step?

THE CYCLE OF REFLECTIVE PRACTICE: THREE CASES

Students, like all people, learn by reflecting on experience.[5] School and classroom experience coalesces around three experience types: academic, personal, and social. Each experience type interacts, complementarily or not, with the other. In rich experiences, such as in a well facilitated project, the three experience types are in full play, likely to dynamically inform each other in ways that result in deeper learning.

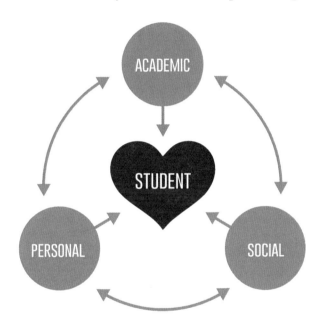

The three experience types are not discrete entities. But by focusing on each, teachers can see the role each has in bringing learning to its fullest potential. If the teacher feels one aspect of experience type is lacking in importance, he or she can give weight to it by making changes to the project. In addition, through the systematic use of reflective practices, students come to realize the importance of the connection between their academic, personal, and social selves.

ACADEMIC REFLECTION

PBL environments are rich in a variety of academic experiences—reading, writing, numeracy, critical thinking, problem solving, design, critique, and presentation. Academic reflections attempt to answer the following questions:

- Who am I as a student?
- How have I grown in this subject or in a particular academic skill?
- What have I learned and what is the significance of what I learned?
- How can I continue to improve in the subject or particular skill?
- How can I better solve problems, make decisions, or complete projects using content and skills relevant to this discipline (i.e., to solve problems as a mathematician, or analyze primary documents as a social scientist)?

HABITS OF MIND

Develop a common set of steps and vocabulary for academic decision making. Post steps and vocabulary in the classroom. Refer to them on a regular basis. Apply them as needed to decision making. One version includes the following practices:

- QUESTION: Ask questions of the material, topic, or problem.
- EVIDENCE: Collect evidence significant to the problem or decision to be made.
- REASON/ANALYSIS: Determine the direction your evidence points. Analyze and arrive at a reason for it.
- CLAIM: State a claim, a conclusion, or course of action.
- CONNECTION/CONSEQUENCES: Make connections to other aspects of the work. Determine the consequences of the claim to the larger context.

THE UPCYCLE
PAT HOLDER, HUMANITIES, AND DAVID BERGGREN, ENGINEERING
HIGH TECH HIGH

*U*pcycling refers to the reuse of discarded objects or material to make a higher quality product. In "The Upcycle," Pat Holder and David Berggren's eleventh grade students approached local non-profit organizations to determine their material needs and designed a product out of upcycled materials that met those needs. Small groups of students built products such as glider launchers, outdoor wash basins, and toy race car ramps, and the students documented their progress, interactions, and thoughts along the way. They published a book chronicling the building, drafts, process notes, and reflections—the foremost being their reflections on academic problem-solving that it took to make the products.

Students and teachers confronted three reflective essential questions:

- What are the environmental and psychological impacts of our personal and consumer cultures rooted in planned obsolescence, materialism and disposability?

- How can engineers define and solve problems while reducing their impacts on the physical environment?

- How can the norms, practices and expectations of culture be challenged through both physical & philosophical efforts?

The Upcycle project incorporates practices of big reflection—reflective opportunities are planned as part of the curriculum, implemented throughout the project, and made into a final product devoted to reasoned, deliberate, and contemplative problem solving. Additionally, it demonstrates the interconnectedness of experiences: while the reflective opportunities published in the students' book are generally about academic experiences related to engineering and the humanities, the project itself also included significant personal and social components.

ACADEMIC REFLECTION IN PRACTICE

REFLECTION ACROSS THE UPCYCLE PROJECT:

Before: What will I do? How will I do it? Why is it important?

Before building their products, students needed to discover the needs of the local non-profits that would be their real-world clients. To this end, in groups of three, students visited a local non-profit, learned more about its mission, and interviewed interested parties. One student group worked with the San Diego Air and Space Museum. They discovered that the education department needed to replace its old glider launchers. Students worked on three different launcher designs and weighed the pros and cons of each before finalizing one. At this point—before the design and build cycles —students wrote answers to the following questions and saved their writing for later publication in *The UpCycle book*:

- Why should we get involved with this organization?
- How did you feel talking to these professionals?
- What are the strengths and weaknesses of your designs? How and why will you chose one over the other designs?

During: What am I doing? How am I doing it? What adjustments can I make?

In the Upcycle Project, this stage of the process involved building the product and maintaining dialogue with the client to ensure that their needs were being met. Students used a variety of tools, including band saws, welding machines, and drill mills, but they did not just use their hands—they regularly paused to think through potential solutions to unforeseen engineering difficulties, they used restorative practices to resolve interpersonal conflicts inside of groups, and they debated solutions to philosophical and social questions raised by their work. Students answered the following questions:

- What challenges in building did you face and how did you solve them?
- Did you have to change your design based on feedback from the client and/or because of the nature of your materials? If so, how?
- Why did you make the design?
- How do you feel about the work so far?
- What is the importance of your work?

After the products were completed and delivered to clients, students put the finishing touches on The Upcycle book— writing of which had started in the "during stage" of the project. At this point, student could now look back on their previous entries to develop their reflections. In addition to these, students also collected design plans, process steps, sketches, and photos to complete the book.

Students were asked to reflect on the following questions:

- What was the environmental impact of the materials before they were upcycled?

- What problems did you encounter and how did you solve or address them? What other solutions were possible? How and why did you choose your solutions?

- What did you learn about yourself?

- What did you learn about the social problem your project work addressed?

THE REFLECTIVE WALK AND TALK

During this stage of the project, when Pat notices that students are getting stuck or frustrated he will often instruct them to go on a "walk and talk." Students go for a walk around the building to discuss their challenge and return with possible solutions. Pat is deliberate to do two things: remove the student from the environment of the problem to give him or her time and space to think (and to remove the class as a potential audience so students can communicate thoughts honestly), and to free the mind to think by getting the body up and moving.

Adam Brown, Math, Computer Science, and Engineering, Dublin High School

The process of having students create projects for outside organizations can be facilitated through this structure. The following protocol prompts students to reflect on their client meetings to refine project goals. It can be adapted to be used for any project in which students address the real needs of individuals or communities.

1. Define the problem being given to you by the client:
   - Summarize in your own words what the client needs.
   - What constraints do you have in addressing those needs?
   - What constraints does your client have?

2. Brainstorm:
   - Brainstorm design ideas based on client needs and and constraints.
   - As a group, decide on your top two ideas.
   - Be prepared to present the pros and cons of each idea to the client.

3. First Presentation to Clients:
   - Clients ask makers (students) to define the problem in the maker's own words. Clients ask follow up questions to ensure that the maker sees the problem in the same way they do and understands their constraints.
   - Makers present their top two design ideas with the pros and cons of each
   - Clients and makers engage in a conversation about the pros and cons of the designs.

4. Develop a Solution:
   - Makers create a detailed design based on client feedback from the presentation. While doing this, students reflect on what is going well, what challenges they face, and how they will solve them.

5. Second Presentation to Clients—Present Solutions:
   - Makers present their final design to the client.
   - Depending on time constraints, the process could end here or continue with as many cycles of product iteration and feedback, as necessary or as time allows.

CONNECTING THE UPCYCLING EXPERIENCES

The Upcycle project contained a heavy academic component—reading about environmental problems and debating their impact on humanity, learning how to design and build as an engineer, and writing an interdisciplinary book—while also interacting with students' personal and social experience. For example, students solved problems in social groups, and learned that academic problems can have social solutions. Or, when students saw the social significance of their engineering product, their work became more meaningful for them personally. It was not just an academic exercise, but a project for a real-word client with a larger social and environmental significance. When students reflected on their experience meeting clients, they saw how their personal choices and experiences inform their academic work. The Upcycle project required the integration of academic, social, and personal experiences, and in so doing, made itself meaningful to the students.

The Upcycle project benefits from the relationship between small and big reflection. Big reflection occurred in key moments planned by the teachers to align with transitional points in the project, and because The Upcycle book required publishable reflective writing. To complement the planned big reflective milestones, teachers took advantage of serendipitous moments and used small reflection organically. Groups of students analyzed their own thinking as needed by the demands of the project or when tension were on the rise for them. In times like these, teachers used a small reflection strategy by asking student to "walk and talk."

PERSONAL REFLECTION

Personal experience refers to the daily lived reality of individuals. For students, personal reflections can refer to large, existential concerns—who am I and where am I going? Or, it can focus on more practical things like personal thoughts about study skills or future goals. A fundamental aspect of schooling is helping students see how different parts of their life relate—how to "figure it all out." Teaching students the interrelationship between their personal, academic, and social experiences is central to this process. By exposing students to a variety of people, situations, and academic endeavors—and providing them with engaging reflective opportunities—students learn that reflection is not just an academic exercise, but a tool for understanding life. Personal reflections often take the form of:

- Who am I?
- What are my passions?
- What am I good at?
- What skills do I need to develop?
- How can I best collaborate with others?
- How can I respect diverse opinions?

PERSONAL REFLECTION IN PRACTICE

THE REFLECTIVE AUTOBIOGRAPHY

Imagine a class in which students partnered with several community organizations to record biographical stories of service from local veterans, and to contribute their stories, photography, and videography to local community centers and a museum. However, in this project, teachers knew that following the community partnership, they would launch a reflective writing project in which students wrote reflective autobiographies. These reflective autobiographies connect their community work with important qualities they value in themselves.

HABITS OF HEART

The habits of heart refer to foundational practices that are inherent to success in school, work, and the community. These complement the habits of the mind found of p. X. There are many variations that can be found online. One version includes the following practices:

- SELF ADVOCACY: Speaking up when confused, holding yourself accountable, and pushing yourself to take new challenges.

- INTELLECTUAL CURIOSITY: Seeking new ideas and unfamiliar perspectives, thinking critically, and asking thought provoking questions.

- INTEGRITY: Grounding actions on an ethical basis, acting responsibly toward your community, and realizing that personal freedom requires personal responsibility.

- COOPERATION: Supporting other individuals in the community, treating peers and adults with respect, and appreciating diversity.

- UNLIMITED POTENTIAL: Being constant learners, making choices with a moral purpose, and remaining open to unexpected possibilities.

Many teachers assign various forms of autobiographies, and with good reason: telling a story of self is a vital step in understanding who one is, and has real value in the world beyond school. Stories of self help friends and family relate to one another and develop a sense of identity and community; sharing a compelling autobiographical statement is a fundamental leadership skill; and (perhaps most notable to high school students and teachers), personal statements are required writing for admission to nearly all four-year colleges and universities in the U.S.

The Reflective Autobiography can happen at any grade level, or any time in the year, but certain grades and times maximize the impact of personal reflection. For example, in the fall semester of twelfth grade, students write personal essays as part of a college application process—they are entering the adult world, and they are making a case for their place in it. In the fall semester of ninth grade, students write personal essays about their identity, their values, and their heroes—they are entering a new academic community, and they are reflecting on their identity as young people and students. In elementary and middle

school, students write personal stories about their hopes and their fears, their family and their friends, their accomplishments and their goals for their lives—they are sharing their identity and considering their many places in the world.

Regardless of the specific grade level or even the name of the assignment, the Reflective Autobiography has common design features that leverage the power of metacognition, self-reflection, and even soul-searching. Like the Upcycle project, the Reflective Autobiography is a project that hinges on big reflection: reflective writing is baked into key elements of the project design.

REFLECTION ACROSS THE REFLECTIVE AUTOBIOGRAPHY PROJECT:

BEFORE—What will I do and how will I do it?

Before writing a Reflective Autobiography, students spend a significant amount of structured time journaling and engaged in reflective discussion about their lives. They reminisce about the past and compare sometimes quite different approaches to life. Teachers should use rituals like a daily journal prompt followed by a pair-share session and then whole class discussion, to establish a safe space and classroom norms for personal reflection. These structured conversations help get the students ready to write. Getting started is often the most difficult part of the writing process—this is true of any kind of writing, but especially true for inward reflection.

Consider prompts such as:

- What is the most significant personal learning experience of your life—in or out of school—and why is it memorable?

- What is the most important lesson that you have learned from a personal hero and why has it stuck with you?

- How can your service learning/community partner/internship site make a valuable contribution to our community?

- What will your contribution to our community be? Why?

- What was your happiest memory? Why?

- What is your saddest memory? Why?

- What was a challenge that you overcame?

- How did you go about doing it?

- Created a diagram mapping out the steps needed to reach their projected goals beyond school.

As students explore their lives for fertile content, they will be inspired by high quality models. All students should read selected personal memoirs and write about vivid moments in their lives inspired by these texts. Provide at least one high quality model that fits well with your students' comfort levels as readers and have each student bring in one sample of a reflective memoir that they respect as an example of a high quality autobiographical text—this can be a speech, poem, song, vignette, or anything similar. If the student examples are songs or anything similar, have them transcribe the words so that they can focus on the writer's use of language. Then, use the critique methods described in Chapter 3 to help students discover and articulate the design principles of high quality reflective autobiographical writing—these become the guideposts for their own work.

During this stage of the project students write their essays. Each journal prompt and each discussion is the raw material—the drafts—needed for students to create one polished draft of a Reflective Autobiography. Situate the students during the writing process so that they can easily access their journals and at least one high quality example of professional or student work—the goal is the create an environment in which students consider their ideas in the context of the type of writing they are trying to create. If this project is done for eleventh or twelfth grade students, focus their writing towards the personal statements required for the Common Application and the University of California prompts. If this project is done in elementary school—or any other context—focus the students' writing on relevant prompts such as "Who is a hero in your eyes, and how can you be a hero also?" or "Imagine yourself 10 years in the future—and write your autobiography."

As students are engaged in the drafting, critique, and revision processes, periodically stop and direct students to write reflectively in their journals. Consider prompts such as:

- What personal discoveries are helping you address our writing prompts?

- What are you noticing about yourself as a writer?

- What are you noticing about yourself as a critique partner?

- How will you decide what to add, take away, or leave the same as you move from this draft to the next?

- How are you doing as an individual within this class?

- How are you doing as a member of this class/community?

Students' final drafts are exhibited for an authentic audience such as (for more on exhibition practices, see Chapter 2):

- High school students send their applications—with these essays—to the college admissions committees (this is high stakes exhibition!), or a mock admissions committee is created for this purpose from community members.

- All students can share their writing with families, or with important community members who influenced their ideas.
- Students can publish a book for themselves that is essentially a class yearbook showcasing their identities and personalities.

Following the student exhibition, students look back at the work they have done and think about what they learned and how they learned. They write a reflective letter to the teacher that responds to prompts such as the following (for more on reflection in the context of student-centered assessment practices, see Chapter 5):

- What did you discover about yourself as a writer? What have you done well as a writer? In your reflection, include an example that provides evidence for your ideas about your accomplishments as a writer.

- What do you need to improve? In your reflection, include an example that provides evidence for your ideas about yourself as a writer who is growing.

- What did you discover about yourself as a character? When you think about your role in the story, what strikes you?

- Describe a moment when you helped someone develop their thoughts about their writing.

- Describe a moment when someone helped you develop your thoughts about your writing.

- How did thinking with others about your life and goals help you complete your story?

- What are you most proud of in this project? Why?

THE ACADEMIC AND SOCIAL VALUE OF PERSONAL REFLECTION:

While The Upcycle project was driven by academic reflection, The Reflective Autobiography is driven by personal reflection. Students are equipped to successfully complete their personal essays because they work together to share and critique their ideas, and also because the stories are about themselves. Such participation demonstrates a fundamental paradox: developing a personal identity is social in nature. Students develop a keener sense of who they are by having their self-conceptions affirmed or challenged by their communities—their points of view become more refined as they are thoughtfully and respectfully questioned by others.

The Reflective Autobiography project does not stop there. Personal experiences influence social and academic experience; when students know themselves better, they better address the issues they face in the social world ("I'm going to be nervous, so I need to practice"). Self understanding has an impact on the academic world, as well. Much of academic success is based on non-cognitive factors such as academic self-perception or tenacity.[6] Personal reflection develops through and informs positive academic and social experiences.

SOCIAL REFLECTION

Social experiences can take many different forms. At the macro level they include institutions and socio-political forces that impact the daily lives of individuals. At the micro level they involve everyday interactions: family life, making a purchase, talking on the phone, or in this instance, the social interactions happening everyday in school and the classroom.

MACRO SOCIO-POLITICAL EXPERIENCE

Socio-political experience refers to a student's relationship to the local community, nation, or world. As Paulo Freire finds in The Pedagogy of the Oppressed, education should be personally and socially transformative. For this to happen, students must be equipped to reflect on the role of social institutions and how those institutions promote or hinder equality and justice. Likewise, students must additionally reflect on their own role in maintaining, ameliorating, or revolutionizing those institutions.

When students reflect on their own socio-political experience they become aware of the various contexts that enmesh their lives. They are subsequently empowered to take action, should they choose, on a variety of local and global issues. Reflection of this nature promotes equity and student voice. When teachers engage students with authentic socio-political reflection, students are empowered to reach their own conclusions.

Reflection of this sort takes the form of the following questions:

- What is happening in my community, my nation, or the world?
- What problems exist in my lived reality that need to be solved and what can we do to help?
- What are the positive qualities of my community that need to be promoted or protected and what can we do to help?
- What social groups or institutions are important in the world around me?
- How can I find out more about, participate in, and positively impact important groups or institutions?

KALE YEAH!
KATE CASALE, YOUTH DEVELOPMENT SPECIALIST
ALAMEDA COUNTY OFFICE OF EDUCATION

Walking through the campus of San Lorenzo High School during lunch on a Tuesday afternoon in the fall of 2016, the casual observer would witness scenes similar to those of many American high schools—students eating spicy hot Cheetos, drinking Monster energy drinks, and consuming various other assorted junk foods. But that same observer would have also seen something out of the ordinary—some students were eating homemade Kale chips, stovetop popcorn, and engaging in campus food activism: they tended to a food stand and sought signatures on a petition drive.

The nine San Lorenzo High School students who organized Kale Yeah! created this event as part of a extra-curricular internship sponsored by Project EAT—a program sponsored by the Alameda County Office of Education. Kale Yeah! was their way of raising awareness about healthy eating in order to persuade other students to sign a petition for the inclusion of a salad bar in the school cafeteria. Kate Casale, their Project EAT internship coordinator, taught them a method of community based research called Youth-Led Participatory Action. The guidelines: to identify major concerns in their schools and communities, conduct research, and propose a course of action—essential skills for any project related to the macro social experience.

Big reflection can develop organically out of students contemplating their social experience (in this case, the food culture of their school). Kale Yeah! works when teachers incorporate student voice and choice into the early stages of project design. Neither students nor teachers went into the project knowing its full shape or how they would share their learning with the community. The idea for a lunchtime food stand and cafeteria petition developed after extensive research,

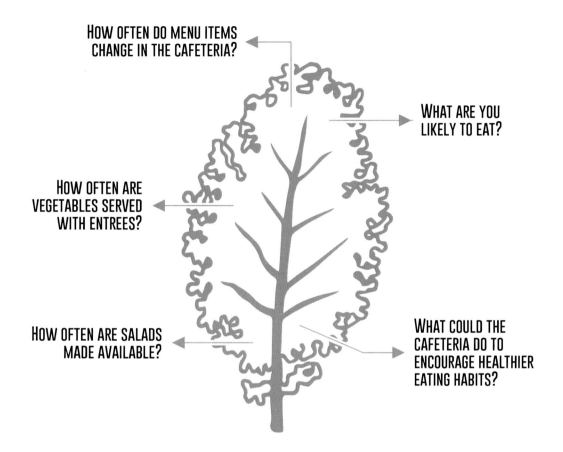

HOW OFTEN DO MENU ITEMS CHANGE IN THE CAFETERIA?

WHAT ARE YOU LIKELY TO EAT?

HOW OFTEN ARE VEGETABLES SERVED WITH ENTREES?

HOW OFTEN ARE SALADS MADE AVAILABLE?

WHAT COULD THE CAFETERIA DO TO ENCOURAGE HEALTHIER EATING HABITS?

reflection, and student-teacher collaboration. It's also a reminder that exhibitions of learning do not have to be singular events; they can be on-going like the food stand. Nor do exhibitions of learning have to be planned during initial project design, they can evolve as the logical action-to-be-taken arising from research and reflection. For more on making student learning public, please see Chapter 2.

SOCIAL REFLECTION IN PRACTICE

REFLECTION ACROSS THE KALE YEAH! PROJECT:

BEFORE—What will I do and how will I do it?

The students who conducted this project believed that there was a problem with the food culture on campus. But what to do about it? Their first step was to develop the guiding question: "Would students make healthier choices if they had more information about the foods they were eating and had healthier options available to them?" Their next step was to map the community by making lunch time observations and conducting student focus groups. This research provided the basis for reflective opportunities which resulted in the formulation of an action plan.

Examples of focus group questions:

- How often do menu items change in the cafeteria?

- How often are vegetables served with entrees?

- How often are salads made available?

- What are you likely to eat? Why?

Examples of cafeteria observation questions:

- What is displayed on the cafeteria televised menu? What's not?

- Is the nutritional information posted in the cafeteria accurate?

- What could the cafeteria do to encourage healthier eating habits?

DURING—What am I doing? How am I doing it? What adjustments can I make?

In this stage, students started with analysis of their research and ended with action. They analyzed data, presented their findings, and made recommendations to the school's ASB. This led student researchers to recommend a petition for a salad bar in the school cafeteria.

In another example, cafeteria observations revealed that students were misinformed or under informed about other food options on or near campus. This led to recommendations for changes in the cafeteria and for an educational campaign on campus. Students took their recommendations and asked, "How can we make this happen?" Questions that guided this stage of the project included:
What were the most important results of our research?

- What recommendations will we make to the ASB based on those findings?

- How can we make those recommendations actionable?

AFTER—What did I do? What did I learn? Where do I go from here?

Students created a post-project report that explained the process and included the results of student reflection. Students asked themselves questions that are common to good post-project reflections:

- What worked? What didn't? Why do I think this?

- How were we challenged?

- How did we succeed?

More specific questions related to the focus groups included:

- Did the focus groups provide accurate data? How do we know?

- Should we have used different questions for the focus groups or reworded them? Why?

- Were the focus group participants being honest? Why do I think this?

KALE YEAH!

Reflection without action is meaningless, but action without reflection may be worse. Not only did the students of *Kale Yeah!* conduct research and reflect on that research, they used their reflections to guide their project. It took courage and faith on the student's part to start a project not knowing where it will go or could go. One could imagine a project like this where students conducted their focus groups, got their data, and moved on.

With *Kale Yeah!* students thought about potential flaws in their data: for example, shy students in the focus groups repeating what the previous person said. In doing so, this became an opportunity for deeper reflection: How do we know what we think we know? How do we create and organize our beliefs? This, in turn creates the context for ongoing metacognitive questioning.

Students learned important lessons about data collection in the social sciences. As a consequence, in future endeavours as researchers, the students will be more aware of potential problems in data collection. As consumers of journalism and in future academic studies, they will be better prepared to look critically at data.

As with the other case studies, *Kale Yeah!* was guided by one particular type of experience, the social, but interconnected with the other two. When Kale Yeah! students reflected on their focus group data, they not only engaged in a macro social experience (the food culture of their school); they concurrently engaged in an academic experience (nutrition studies, conducting a focus group and analyzing data) and personally, in thinking about their own eating habits.

THE MICRO SOCIAL EXPERIENCE:

A large part of what happens in school is social. Micro social experience here refers to the daily interactions amongst students and between students and adults. These interactions provide opportunities for students to learn how to get along with one another and to help one another learn. Furthermore, classrooms develop unique personalities that can turn in different directions on the actions of individual students, groups of students, and/or the teacher.

The purpose of micro social reflection is to increase awareness of these dynamics. The group level (what "we" do) can have significant impact for the individual within the group (what "I" do). In many cases, the peer group can be said to have as much impact, if not more, than anything else. Micro social reflections often take the following form:

- How well did your group work together?

- How well did you contribute to the group?

- Are you doing too much of the work or too little?

- How could you have encouraged other people to participate in this conversation?

- What did you learn from other people?

Facilitating micro social reflection can be powerful way of promoting deeper academic learning for all students. Maintaining positive classroom rapport, cultivating positive emotions in the room, engaging productively in interesting work, and listening to student voice and choice all help. Structuring more formal experiences in which students learn they are not alone in the experience helps students navigate a change in thought pattern from "we are having a problem with x" to "We can overcome that problem by ..."

Proactive circles provide a way for students to arrive at this.[7] They were designed by the International Institute of Restorative Practices to prevent social problems before they arise. Frequently used as an empathy building exercise to address social challenges in the classroom, they also provide structured opportunities for students to address academic issues related to the project. Proactive circles work especially well after exhibition or project completion, by structuring opportunities for students to debrief high stakes events in a supportive social environment.

THE PROACTIVE CIRCLE STEPS

1. Students set up the classroom in a circle with everyone in the same type of chair.

2. Students use a talking stick. Students are only allowed to share if they hold the talking stick.

3. Discussion norms are reviewed (e.g. no sidebar conversations, no laughter, no confrontation).

4. The facilitator proceeds with prepared questions meant to take the social, emotional, and academic temperature of the class, the questions are:

   ○ How are you feeling right now?

   ○ What is something you learned these past couple of weeks?

   ○ What is something that challenged you this week?

   ○ What is something you want to celebrate or are proud of?

   ○ What is a goal you have for yourself and why?

5. To close the circle, students ask questions, share final thoughts and feelings, or pass.

While the micro social experience takes place in the classroom, if greater value to the student's social experience is to occur, then the "outside world's" macro social experience must enter into the room. Simply working at the micro level is not enough to make a project socially viable. In the Kale Yeah! project students participated actively in the social world both at the micro level (working with their peers in project delivery) and at a macro level (cafeteria food choices and lunch-time activism). In doing so, the project's rich social experience, at both the macro and micro levels, made the academic work more important and personally empowered students to do something important.

Reflection should not be tacked on to a project or unit as a quick afterthought. Instead, reflective practices should be used as ongoing processes that inform the next step and places significance upon what has already happened. Reflection operates best when it becomes a mindset that is reinforced throughout the project and moves beyond it as well.

Unfortunately, however, it may seem expedient to bypass or rush through reflection during the hurly burly of project deadlines and unforeseen circumstances. This is especially true towards the end of a project, when students and teachers are in a frenzied state of preparation before an exhibition event and exhausted afterward. Teachers should be mindful of this while not being discouraged. Place buffers in the calendar—before, during, and after important project work—that create time for reflection. In addition, be prepared with reflective go-to questions that can settle nerves or take advantage of serendipity. By taking time to think, the teacher can save time by making the next step the easier for it.

If reflection is not part of the project, teachers can fall into the very trap that they are trying to avoid: failing to authentically and meaningfully engage students. Through poor planning, bad luck, or misguided priorities we might avoid "teaching to the test" only to replace it with a single minded focus on "teaching to the product." In other words, teachers can get stuck in a pattern where meeting project benchmarks and completing the final product becomes the PBL version of racing through curriculum in order to score highly on a standardized test. By stopping to reflect, teachers can remind students that making a product is a process and that learning occurs by reflecting on that process.

Conversely, as with all good things, it is possible to have too much reflection. If reflection becomes a repetitive chore for students, with nothing new or important surfacing, it will lose its power. If big reflections don't connect to the goals of the project or if small reflections fail to take advantage of developments or unforeseen opportunities, students will not see their purpose.

All three of this chapter's cases demonstrate that academic, personal, and social reflection must interact for deeper learning to occur. If any one of the three experience types is diminished then learning is diminished. When the student's personal experience is confrontive or difficult, discomfort grows, and engagement in learning lost. When the student's social experience is assumed or neglected, team cohesiveness is damaged and students become disengaged from the real world significance of their work. Academic experience in itself requires social significance and the student's own personal interest.

Understanding the importance of rich and fully integrating experiences places a final expectation on the project. The right balance of small and big reflection creates flexibility, and students working in PBL environments will recognize how their academic, personal, and social experiences can either support or interfere with learning. They will, in other words, take one more step in the life long process of knowing themselves.

1. Alec Patton, *Work That Matters: The Teacher's Guide to Project-Based Learning* (London: Paul Hamlyn Foundation, 2012).

2. "High Tech High Schools—Education Design Kit," HTH Graduate School of Education, accessed May 15, 2017, http://gse.hightechhigh.org/design/essential_question.php.

3. Joseph P. McDonald, Nancy Mohr, Alan Dichter, and Elizabeth C. McDonald, The *Power of Protocols: An Educator's Guide to Better Practice* (Moorabbin, Australia: Hawker Brownlow Education), 2013.

4. "High Tech High Schools—Education Design Kit."

CHAPTER 2

1. "High Tech High Schools—Education Design Kit."

2. "Presentations of Learning," Share Your Learning, accessed May 12, 2017, http://www.shareyourlearning.org/pol/. High Tech High is working with several organizations to create a practitioner hub for deeper learning practices. The content found at shareyourlearning.org comes from HTH staff, in collaboration with staff at other schools in the deeper learning network.

3. "Presentations of Learning."

4. "Student Led Conference," Share Your Learning, accessed May 12, 2017, http://www.shareyourlearning.org/SLC/.

CHAPTER 3

1. "Interview with Rob Riordan." Interview by author. January 26, 2017.

2. "HTH GSE | Education Design Kit." HTH Graduate School of Education. Accessed May 15, 2017. http://gse.hightechhigh.org/design/critique.php.

3. Ron Berger, *An ethic of excellence: building a culture of craftsmanship with students.* Portsmouth, NH: Heinemann, 2003.

4. Ron Berger, *An ethic of excellence: building a culture of craftsmanship with students.* Portsmouth, NH: Heinemann, 2003.

5. Joseph P. McDonald, Nancy Mohr, Alan Dichter, and Elizabeth C. McDonald. *The power of protocols: an educator's guide to better practice.* Moorabbin, Vic.: Hawker Brownlow Education, 2013.

6. "Interview with Ron Berger." Interview by author. March 15, 2017.

7. "Interview with Rob Riordan." Interview by author. January 26, 2017.

8. Kelly Gallagher, "Making the Most of Mentor Texts," *Educational Leadership* 17, no. 7 (2014): 28–33, accessed May 15, 2017, http://www.ascd.org/publications/educational-leadership/apr14/vol71/num07/Making-the-Most-of-Mentor-Texts.aspx.

9. Ron Berger, *An Ethic of Excellence: Building a Culture of Craftsmanship with Students* (Portsmouth, NH: Heinemann), 2003.

10. "Interview with Ron Berger." Interview by author. March 15, 2017.

11. "Interview with Ron Berger." Interview by author. March 15, 2017.

CHAPTER 4

1. "What Is Service Learning?," Corporation for National & Community Service. AmeriCorps, June 21, 2011, accessed February 2, 2017, https://www.nationalservice.gov/.

2. "Intuitions Confirmed. The Bottom-Line Return on School-to-Work Investment for Students and Employers," National Employer Leadership Council, 1999, accessed May 12, 2017, http://files.eric.ed.gov/fulltext/ED430083.pdf.

3. "Intuitions Confirmed." A second study conducted by the US Department of Education's Office of Educational Research and Improvement focuses on the implications of school-to-work programs in one San Rafael, California, company. See Lauri J. Bassi, Theresa Feeley, John Hillmyer, and Jens Ludwig, "Learning and Earning: An Employer's Look at School-to-Work Investments," American Society for Training and Development, 1997, accessed May 12, 2017, https://www.td.or.

4. Rob Riordan, personal interview, January 25, 2017.

5. Excerpted from Lili Allen, Christopher J. Hogan, and Adria Steinberg, *Knowing and Doing: Connecting Learning and Work* (Providence, RI: Northeast and Islands Regional Educational Laboratory at Brown University, 2000).

CHAPTER 5

1. "High Tech High Schools—Education Design Kit."

2. "North, South, East and West: Compass Points," National School Reform Faculty, Harmony Education Center, https://www.nsrfharmony.org/system/files/protocols/north_south_0.pdf.

3. Elizabeth G. Cohen and Rachel A. Lotan, "Producing Equal-Status Interaction in the Heterogeneous Classroom," *American Educational Research Journal* 32, no. 1 (2016): 99–120.

4. Randy Scherer, "How To," *Ampersand: The Student Journal of School & Work*, February 5, 2014, accessed June 12, 2017, https://sites.google.com/a/hightechhigh.org/ampersand/how-to.

5. "High Tech High Schools—Education Design Kit"; Scherer, "How To."

6. Austin Kleon, *Show Your Work! 10 Ways to Share Your Creativity and Get Discovered* (New York: Workman Publishing, 2014).

CHAPTER 6

1. Donna Wilson, "Metacognition: The Gift That Keeps Giving," Edutopia, October 7, 2014, accessed May 15, 2017, https://www.edutopia.org/blog/metacognition-gift-that-keeps-giving-donna-wilson-marcus-conyers.

2. Mary Helen Yang-Immordino, *Emotions, Learning, and the Brain: Exploring the Educational Implications of Affective Neuroscience* (New York: Norton, 2016), 43.

3. Yang-Immordino, Emotions, Learning, and the Brain, p. 43.

4. Jeffrey D. Karpicke, "Retrieval-Based Learning: Active Retrieval Promotes Meaningful Learning," *Current Directions in Psychological Science* 21 no. 3 (2012): 157–63, http://learninglab.psych.purdue.edu/downloads/2012_Karpicke_CDPS.pdf.

5. David A. Kolb, *Experiential Learning: Experience as the Source of Learning and Development.* Englewood Cliffs, NJ: Prentice Hall, 1984.

6. Carol S. Dweck, Gregory M. Walton, and Geoffrey L. Cohen, "Academic Tenacity: Mindsets and Skills that Promote Long-Term Learning," Bill & Melinda Gates Foundation, 2014, https://ed.stanford.edu/sites/default/files/manual/dweck-walton-cohen-2014.pdf.

7. "Defining Restorative: 5.2. Circles," International Institute for Restorative Practices, accessed June 12, 2017, http://www.iirp.edu/what-we-do/what-is-restorative-practices/defining-restorative/21-5-2-circles.

ADDITIONAL RESOURCES

Abeles, V. *Beyond Measure: Rescuing an Overscheduled, Overtested, Underestimated Generation.* New York: Simon & Schuster, 2015.

Alber, Rebecca. "Using Mentor Texts to Motivate and Support Student Writers." Edutopia, July 31, 2014. https://www.edutopia.org/blog/using-mentor-text-motivate-and-support-student-writers-rebecca-alber.

Ampersand: The Student Journal of School & Work. Home page. https://sites.google.com/a/hightechhigh.org/ampersand/.

Berger, R. *An Ethic of Excellence: Building a Culture of Craftsmanship with Students* (Portsmouth, NH: Heinemann), 2003.

Berger, Ron, Leah Rugen, and Libby Woodfin. *Leaders of Their Own Learning: Transforming Schools through Student-Engaged Assessment.* San Francisco, CA: Jossey-Bass, 2014.

Berger, Ron, Libby Woodfin, and Anne Vilen. *Learning That Lasts: Challenging, Engaging, and Empowering Students with Deeper Instruction.* San Francisco, CA: Jossey-Bass & Pfeiffer Imprints, Wiley, 2016.

Briceno, E. "Mindsets and Student Agency." *UnBoxed* 10 (Spring 2013). http://www.hightechhigh.org/unboxed/issue10/.

Cohen, Elizabeth, and Rachel Lotan. *Designing Groupwork: Strategies for the Heterogeneous Classroom.* 3rd ed. New York: Teachers College Press, 2014.

Cushman, Kathleen. *Fires in the Mind.* New York: New Press, 2003.

Dewey, J. *Experience and Education.* New York: Simon & Schuster Touchstone Edition, 1997. First published 1938 by Kappa Delta Pi.

Freire, Paulo. "Reprint: Cultural Action for Freedom." *Harvard Educational Review* 68 no. 4 (December 1998): 476–22.

Gallagher, Kelly. "Making the Most of Mentor Texts." *Educational Leadership* 17, no. 7 (2014): 28–33. http://www.ascd.org/publications/educational-leadership/apr14/vol71/num07/Making-the-Most-of-Mentor-Texts.aspx.

Heath, C., and D. Heath. *Switch: How to Change Things When Change Is Hard.* New York: Random House, 2011.

High Tech High Schools—Education Design Kit. Home page. http://gse.hightechhigh.org/design

Jana, Peter, and Daisy Sharrock. "Unraveling the Knot: Critical Thinking in Presentations of Learning." *UnBoxed* 9 (Fall 2012). https://gse.hightechhigh.org/unboxed/issue9/critical_thinking_in_presentations_of_learning/.

Krueger, B. "Students as Experts in Professional Development." *UnBoxed* 11 (Spring 2014). http://www.hightechhigh.org/unboxed/issue11/students_as_experts_in_professional_development/.

Patton, A. *Work That Matters: The Teacher's Guide to Project-Based Learning* (London: Paul Hamlyn Foundation, 2012).

Pink, D. *Drive: The Surprising Truth about What Motivates Us.* New York: Riverhead Books, 2011.

Riordan, R. and L. Rosenstock. "Changing the Subject." Monograph, High Tech High Graduate School of Education, 2013. http://gse.hightechhigh.org/.

Ruff, J. "Collaboration, Critique, and Classroom Culture." *UnBoxed* 6 (Fall 2010). http://gse.hightechhigh.org/unboxed/issue6/editors_welcome.php.

Scherer, Randy. "Exhibiting Student Writing." *UnBoxed* 7 (Spring 2011). https://gse.hightechhigh.org/unboxed/issue7/exhibiting_student_writing/.

Scherer, Randy. "Every Classroom Should Be a Maker Space." *UnBoxed* 14 (Fall 2015). http://gse.hightechhigh.org/unboxed/issue14/every_classroom_should_be_a_maker_space/.

Students at High Tech High Media Arts. *Ampersand: The Student Journal of School & Work.* Vol. 7. San Diego, CA: High Tech High Media Arts, 2015.

UnBoxed. Home page. http://gse.hightechhigh.org/unboxed/.

Wagner, Tony, and Ted Dintersmith. *Most Likely to Succeed: Preparing Our Kids for the Innovation Era.* New York: Scribner, 2015.

ALEC PATTON, PH.D.

Alec teaches humanities at High Tech High Chula Vista, and before that, at High Tech High North County. Alec first became interested in project-based learning when he was doing his PhD at the University of Sheffield. Prior to joining High Tech High, Alec worked in London, at the Innovation Unit, a non-profit company that works with the people who provide public services to help them find innovative solutions to difficult problems. While he was working at the Innovation Unit, Alec wrote and/or edited several publications about innovative education around the world, including Work That Matters.

KELLY WILLIAMS

Kelly Williams was born and raised in Texas and earned her B.A. in English, Language, and Literature as well as her Masters in Teaching from the University of Virginia. While in college, Kelly also played for four years on the Virginia women's varsity soccer team earning the role of captain her senior year. After graduating, she taught English classes and coached soccer at comprehensive high schools in Jacksonville, FL and Poway, CA. Then she found her way to project-based learning and High Tech High where she has spent the last eight years of her career. When not in the classroom, Kelly loves spending time with her husband, two children, and Rhodesian Ridgeback. She can usually be found exploring the great outdoors with her family.

MICHELLE SADRENA CLARK

Michelle Sadrena Clark is a ninth grade World Cultures, Geography, and Literature teacher at High Tech High North County in San Marcos, California and a School Transformation Coach. She earned her Master's in Pacific International Affairs at the Graduate School of International Relations and Pacific Studies, University of California, San Diego, with a concentration in International Development and a specialization in Latin America. Prior to graduate school, Michelle lived in Bisai, Japan for two years, teaching English and American culture at public junior high schools while engaging in performance dance and theater. Michelle received her undergraduate degree at the University of California, Irvine, with a major in International Studies and a minor in Clinical Psychology. During

251

this time she also attended La Universidad Catolica Pontificia in Santiago, Chile for one semester. Her speaking engagements include the USC Shoah Foundation Gala when Stephen Spielberg presented President Barack Obama with the Ambassador for Humanity Award, TEDx Hollywood, and the Past is Present 70th commemoration of the liberation of Auschwitz. Michelle is a student in the Joint Doctoral Program in Educational Leadership at the University of California, San Diego and California State University, San Marcos.

COLLEEN GREEN, PH.D.

Colleen is a native of Michigan and has called San Diego home for the last 12 years. Colleen has worked in the HTH organization for over a decade. She began as an 11th and 12th grade humanities teacher at the Gary and Jerri-Ann Jacobs HTH before becoming the founding school director of High Tech High Chula Vista, where she spent four years. Colleen then served as director of High Tech High International. Following that, Colleen was excited to return to the classroom, to teach English at HTHI. Colleen has taught in South Africa as a Teach with Africa fellow, working with students and teachers in Ga Rankuwa at Leap 6. Colleen has her undergraduate from Grand Valley State University, her Masters from Bowling Green State University and her Ph.D. through Purdue University.

SARAH STRONG

Sarah Strong has worked in the High Tech High organization for eleven years. Her passion is using the math classroom to help students find joy and value in doing work that matters. She teaches high school math classes and coaches teachers, helping them dream about what their classrooms could look and feel like, particularly in the area of student voice in projects and assessment. She has worked at three of the High Tech schools, teaching middle and high school math and science. Raised in the San Francisco Bay Area, Sarah moved to San Diego in 2001 to attend Point Loma Nazarene University where she earned a BS in Mathematics and her teaching credential. She was a member of the inaugural cohort of the Teacher Leadership Program in the High Tech High Graduate School of Education where she explored student experiences with open-ended math problems in 2009.

PETER JANA

Peter Jana is a San Diego native who was educated at San Diego State University and the Claremont Graduate School. Peter has lived in Paris, France. and taught on deployed Navy warships as a community college instructor. Peter has taught Humanities for thirteen years at The Gary and Jerri-Ann Jacobs High Tech High and taught reading and writing methods and the philosophy of education for the HTH credentialing program.

TOM FEHERENBACHER

Tom Fehrenbacher began teaching at Hoover High School in San Diego in 1990. Working on the Restructuring Steering Committee there, he helped with Hoover's transition to the Coalition of Essential Schools. When the New Urban High School Project selected Hoover as a member, Tom participated in the effort to distill best practices in internships, career stands, and digital portfolios. In 2003, Tom Fehrenbacher joined the faculty of High Tech High, teaching 11th grade humanities. Over the next ten years, Tom integrated humanities with his partner in biology, Dr. Jay Vavra. During their years together, the team completed a series of published San Diego Bay Field Guides. Currently, Tom contributes to staff development efforts through in-services on the student critique process, collegial coaching, neuroscience of emotions and learning, and school reform. Tom has taught credentialing classes in "Reading and Writing Across the Curriculum," "Advanced Humanities Methods," and "The Philosophy of Education."

RANDY SCHERER

Randy Scherer directs the California Career Pathways PBL Leadership Academy, a professional development program developed in conjunction with the California Department of Education Career Pathways Trust. Prior to that, Randy taught humanities at High Tech High Media Arts for ten years, where we was a founding member of the faculty. Randy was a founding member and editor of UnBoxed: A Journal of Adult Learning in Schools. He has developed and presented workshops centered on project based learning and school reform for educators and policy makers in the US and abroad. Before joining the HTH Village of schools, Randy was the production manager for three national magazines in New York City, and while teaching Randy published four nonfiction books. Randy received his B.A. in Political Science and English from Binghamton University, his teaching credential from the University of San Diego and his M.Ed. in Teacher Leadership from the High Tech High Graduate School of Education.

ACKNOWLEDGEMENTS

Creating *Hands and Minds: A Guide to Project-Based Learning for Teachers by Teachers* and the accompanying volume *Inspiration, Not Replication: How Teachers Are Leading School Change From the Inside*, would not have been possible without the support of a diverse community of passionate educators, students, and professionals across the state of California, the United States, and beyond.

We sincerely appreciate the dedicated professionals at the California Career Pathways Trust and the California Department of Education. Thank you to Abby Medina, Joe Radding, Karen Shores, Christine Hess, Russ Weikle, and Donna Wyatt, whose support was essential to this work.

We express our gratitude to Larry Rosenstock and Rob Riordan, High Tech High co-founders, who provided seemingly endless and invaluable insight into the pursuit of equity in education; Brent Spirnak, whose videography and photography was vital to the research that went into this project, and can be found online at hightechhigh.org; Enrique Lugo, for his creative vision and providing the graphic design that brings this book to life; Carmen Ramirez for supporting this project at every step; Felicia Hamway, Justine Aldridge, Kristy Renken, Kay McElrath, and Jenny Salkeld for ensuring sound business practices; and to Stephen Hamilton and Tom Fehrenbacher for editing these publications.

We are indebted to the teams of HTH Team Mentors who shared their endless passion and expertise for this work and who supported the PBL Leadership Academy teams: Emily Carter, Tina Chavez, Alicia Crump, Georgia Figueroa, Andrew Gloag, Kelly Jacob, Julia Jacobson, Mari Jones, Shani Leader, Charlie Linnik, Don MacKay, Jeremy Manger, Maggie Miller, Rachel Nichols, Mark Poole, Zoe Randall, John Santos, Mele Sato, Mackenzie Schultz, David Smith, and Janna Steffan.

We could not have completed this without the broader community of HTH educators at all schools and all grade levels. Many thanks to Mark Aguirre, Sarah Barnes, Cate Challen, Tina Chavez, Corey Clark, Ben Daley, Janie Griswold, Jessica Hoffman, Pat Holder, Jamelle

Jones, Chris Olivas, Kaleb Rashad, Juli Ruff, Jesse Wade-Robinson, Kelly Wilson, and Jade White.

Thank you to the guest faculty who lent their time, expertise, and boundless energy towards the PBL Leadership Academy: Ron Berger, Ashanti Branch, Victor Diaz, Albert Yu Min Lin, Emily Pilloton, Katie Rast, Tony Simmons, Adria Steinberg, Elliot Washor, and Yong Zhao.

We could not have produced these volumes without the educators who graciously opened their schools, classrooms, and hearts to us: the students from Windsor High School who shared their insider view of project-based learning and provided valuable advice on project design with Sonoma teachers during the C3 Project Based Learning Institute—and to Chuck Wade, Jessica Progulske, and the Sonoma County Office of Education team that made it possible; Dawn Miller of the Lindsay Community School, San Diego, for providing an exemplary model of how to provide students with rich social experiences; Erica Palicki, Samantha Howerton, and Dorothy Corona from S.O.A.R. Academy East Mesa; Matt Simon and the entire Momentum Learning team across San Diego County; Adam Brown from the Dublin School in Dublin, CA, for contributing effective strategies for employing academic reflection in engineering classes; Kate Casale of the Alameda County Office of Education; Lorilee Niessen of the Capital Region Academies for the Next Economy (CRANE), who shared her expertise, time, and resources, and took our writers from school to school to see first-hand about how they are transforming the teacher and student experience via PBL; The entire team at Central Coast New Tech High School, and Jennifer Isbell and Jennifer Stillittano for taking time for extensive interviews and providing valuable resources; the engineering department from Dublin High School in the Bay Area; "The PBL Team" at Anderson Valley Junior Senior High School; Joshua Dresser at Chicago Tech Academy; and Tammie Halloway at Napa County Office of Education.

We extend a deep thank you to the many fantastic, creative, and tireless educators who we worked with from the following schools, districts, and counties: Academy of the Canyons Middle College High School; Alameda County Office Of Education; Anderson Valley Unified School District; Antelope Valley Community College; Assurance Learning Academy; Capital Region Academies for the Next Economy (CRANE); Centinela Valley Union High School District; Contra Costa County Office of Education; Coronado Unified School District; Delhi Unified School District; Diego Valley Charter School; Downey

Unified School District; Fresno Unified School District; Glendale Unified School District; Grossmont High School; Inglewood Unified School District; John Muir Charter Schools; Konocti Unified School District; Liberty Ranch High School; Livermore Valley Joint Unified School District; Los Angeles Unified School District; Mariposa County Unified School District; Momentum Learning schools including the Lindsay School, North County Community Schools, South County Community Schools, the Monarch School, S.O.A.R. Academy East Mesa; Montebello Unified School District; Napa County Office of Education; Northern Humboldt Union High School District; Orange County Department of Education; Oxnard Union High School District; Placentia–Yorba Linda School District; Paramount Career Prep Academy; San Luis Obispo Community College District; San Luis Obispo County Office of Education; Santa Clarita Community College School District; Shasta College; Solano County Office of Education; Sonoma County Office of Education; Sutter County Office of Education; Tulare County Office of Education; Ventura County Office of Education; Victor Valley College; Visalia Unified School District; W.E.B. DuBois Public Charter School; West Placer Unified School District; West Valley College; Yosemite Community College District.

We are thankful for the support of the following educational organizations: Big Picture Learning, EL Learning, the National Writing Project, New Tech Network for supporting this work.

Thank you to Karen Beretsky for her patience and encouragement during long weekends of writing and editing; Mamba Clark, Sasha Clark, Dwight Pledger, Sadie Pledger; Sara Freedman, Web Communications Specialist, Oregon State University Cascades; and Lauri Scherer for invaluable support and editorial guidance. We are forever grateful to all of our families for supporting this work.

Made in the USA
Monee, IL
17 September 2022

14121172R00155